GOOD BIRDERS
STILL DON'T WEAR WHITE

GOOD BIRDERS
STILL DON'T WEAR WHITE

SEE
BIRDS

Passionate Birders Share
the Joys of Watching Birds

EDITED BY

LISA A. WHITE

AND

JEFFREY A. GORDON

ILLUSTRATED BY

ROBERT A. BRAUNFIELD

HOUGHTON MIFFLIN HARCOURT
BOSTON • NEW YORK • 2017

Library of Congress Cataloging-in-Publication Data is available.
ISBN 978-0-544-87609-5

Book design by Eugenie S. Delaney

Printed in the United States of America
DOC 10 9 8 7 6 5 4 3 2 1

Like birds?
We can help with that!

The American Birding Association is dedicated to making birding better for all. We invite you to come explore the wealth of useful, fun, and free resources we offer to all birders, as well as the many additional benefits of ABA membership.

Go to **aba.org/goodbirders** and get started today.

CONTENTS

Contents

Contents

INTRODUCTION

by Jeffrey A. Gordon

"I'M GOING TO LOOK FOR A YELLOW-HEADED BLACKBIRD."
The speaker was thirteen-year-old me, having begun really paying attention to birds only a year or so before. Now, forty years later, I'm still amazed and even a little embarrassed at what a brash declaration this really was. To the adults present when I said it, I'm certain it sounded utterly ridiculous, but they were too kind to say so. Really, there was no need. Experience would teach me, as it had taught them. But experience had a very different lesson planned for that morning.

It was September, and members of the Delmarva Ornithological Society had gathered for a field trip to Dragon Run Marsh near Delaware City, Delaware. I was not only by far the youngest and most unseasoned person in the group, I was armed. Armed with a brand-new spotting scope, a powerful instrument that my mentor wryly cautioned would merely allow me to misidentify birds that were farther away, if I wasn't careful. So when I saw a flock of several dozen blackbirds, mostly red-winged, leapfrogging through the cattails that lined the distant shore of the impoundment where we were birding, I immediately set about deploying my shiny new weaponry to inspect them.

There was nothing unusual in any of this. Birders commonly sift through flocks, sometimes very large flocks, be they blackbirds, gulls, shorebirds, geese—almost any concentration of birds—in large part because they hope to find something different, maybe something rare. There wasn't even anything too crazy in having a fleeting microfantasy that those red-wings might have a far out-of-place yellow-headed—a spectacular western species that I'd seen only in pictures—among them. We all have thousands of improbable thoughts, notions, dreams, and fragments thereof that pass through our minds more or less constantly. "Surely that knife blade isn't as sharp as they say it is." "I can jump that." "I don't see any cops around—let's go for it!"

Those of us who wish to avoid embarrassment, injury, and/or incarceration wisely let these little thoughtlets pass unremarked and certainly unacted upon. What was nuts was not that I thought that day about finding a yellow-headed blackbird. It was that I opened my mouth and said so loudly and with a complete lack of sarcasm. It's not unlike announcing on the tee that one is about to sink a hole in one, no big deal, and does anybody want to bet a hundred bucks that I won't? Sure, everyone has those few milliseconds when that exact idea flashes across your mind. But say so out loud and in earnest and you will quickly lose all your credibility, your money, and any future golfing invitations, in that order.

Aware of those stakes as I was—and despite their reputation for recklessness, teenagers are keenly aware of any risk of shame or disgrace—I still went ahead and blurted out my avian intentions for all to hear.

And the birding gods, instead of laughing at me, decided to honor my petition. Perhaps the fourth or fifth bird that I looked at was none other than a yellow-headed blackbird. And not just a brownish juvenile with a mustard stain across its throat, but a searingly gorgeous adult male, resplendent and perfect.

"I found one. A yellow-headed blackbird!" I said. A dozen heads whipped around, and a dozen faces stared at me agog.

At that point, things could have really gone south. I could have announced my find, only to have the bird drop from view into the vegetation, never to be refound. But instead my incredible good fortune held, and the bird stayed put, granting everyone in the group the chance to take their turn at the scope and to marvel at his incandescence. Then he flew off, leaving those birder heads and faces beaming and shaking in wonder and disbelief.

I wish I could say that that was the day I discovered I had superpowers, an ability to summon birds out of thin air merely by speaking their names. Alas, no. In the thousands of mornings afield that have followed, I have learned, as my adult companions that day already knew, that rare birds really are pretty rare, and that big talk will make you a fool far more often than it will make you a hero.

But that day did teach me a number of really key things. Most crucially, it showed me that I, barely out of elementary school, had found a community in which I could make a positive and valued contribution. I could do things that surprised and delighted people—that made them feel happy and grateful. That's an all too rare feeling for most of us, even as adults. For me, as a struggling, often awkward adolescent, it was transformative.

Of course, it wasn't just a lucky prediction about a rare blackbird that made that transformation happen, though that certainly serves as a lovely and memorable signpost. It was discovering that birders as a tribe functioned in ways that were different and in most ways superior to the *Lord of the Flies* world of junior high school that was then my day-to-day reality.

For starters, birders were smart and curious. They liked solving puzzles and having command of a large number of facts. They paid attention to the natural world and its daily, seasonal, and annual cycles. They knew geography at an unusual level of detail, regularly visiting places that few knew existed. Birds, the objects of their passion, were real and nearly omnipresent, yet seemed to belong to another world, one full of color and flight and mystery and the raw drama of survival.

I think that even more than all these, what really drew me into the community was that birders had a code. A code of honor and conduct and ethics that, while largely unwritten, was known and for the most part closely observed by all. It emphasized being open to all: what you looked like, how much money you had, or what your job title was—indeed, most traditional markers of status—were far less important than your interest and ability in finding and identifying birds.

An even more important value involved being honest and reliable. In birding, you are as good as your word. If you're not sure that you saw a certain bird, you're expected to say so. Well-intentioned mistakes are forgiven, even valued as learning opportunities, as long as they are openly admitted. But dishonesty will get you shunned, fast.

But it was probably birders' unique generosity and ethic of sharing that impressed me most. I've heard dogs described as compulsive greeters. Without doubt, an ecstatic, tail-wagging greeting is the cornerstone of canine society. In a similar way, birders might be said to be compulsive sharers. They always want to know what birds you've seen recently, and which ones you're hoping to see in the future, and they'll let you know what's on their list and on their wish list. Come upon another birder in the field, and it's expected that each of you will share with the other any leads or tidbits of information you may have, almost without exception. Most birders get a deep sense of satisfaction from helping others see and enjoy birds.

Compare this to, say, fishing, where anglers are typically quite guarded about the precise locations they go and techniques they use. Before I get deluged with hate mail, let me clarify that I am also a fisherman, and I fully realize that anglers can be quite generous. But it's not the same and not to the same extent as it is with birders.

It only makes sense, though, when you consider that anglers, even those who practice catch and release, are competing for a scarce resource. Somebody always catches the biggest fish, or the most fish, or the rarest fish, one at a time. Birds, on the other hand, are better when shared. If you see a cool bird, great. If you show it to some friends and family, so much the better. Heck, you could even bring a whole school bus loaded with kids over to look at it, or a bird club field trip group, and as long as you're careful not to disturb the bird or its habitat unduly, everybody wins. There just aren't that many hobbies where the same can be said.

I find this same spirit of generosity, honesty, and passionate interest in the world to be as strong today as it was nearly half a century ago. You'll find it strong, too, as you read through the essays in this book, which were written by birders with startlingly different personalities, life experiences, and areas of interest.

You'll find many people writing paeans to the birds and places and techniques they love, that bring them reward year after year. Steve Howell loves Mexico. Corey Finger loves

New York. Amar Ayyash loves gulls. Nick Lund loves tacos. Debi Shearwater . . . well, you get the idea.

You'll find some nicely contrasting takes on things like bird song, which Tom Stephenson and Nathan Pieplow approach from a scientific direction but which Bill Thompson III comes at through his and his family's lifelong love of making music. Yet all three are clearly in awe of the beauty, of the aesthetic form and ecological function of bird sounds.

Sophie Webb, Catherine Hamilton, and Marie Read are all bird artists, the first two painters and the latter a photographer, but all three underline the value of time spent observing birds in the field that their art demands.

Donna Dittmann and Ioana Seritan both extol the wonders of bird collections in museums, and how a knowledge of the specimens there informs their appreciation and understanding of these most vital and vibrant of Earth's creatures.

Dorian Anderson and J. Drew Lanham ponder the relationship of birders to hunters, Dorian finding kinship where he hadn't expected it, and Drew, who is both a hunter and a birder, examining how both approaches have informed his view of his place in the world and the person he is.

Ted Floyd and Julie Zickefoose tell us how birding has enriched and strengthened their bond with their children, while Jennie Duberstein tells how birding can soften seemingly insurmountable cultural barriers between people of wildly diverse backgrounds. Kenn Kaufman, as expert and experienced a birder as has ever lived, emphasizes the value of giving aid to those just taking their first steps down the birding path, whatever their age and relationship to you.

And through it all, Rob Braunfield's delightful and incisive drawings capture many of the feelings of the authors, and of all of us who love birds and birding.

Taken as a whole, these people and their essays tell a story of birding as a way of finding one's place in the world, of figuring out where we, as individual people and as a species, fit in. Of keeping one's eyes open even when that gets a little tough, and maintaining a sense of humor and a healthy skepticism about it all. Of honoring your own experiences and honoring those of others.

For me, birding has been and continues to be all of these things. In the company of birders, I have time and again seen the best of humanity. I've found far more than just the thrill of discovering the rare and the beautiful, as I did with that brilliant blackbird on a September morning so long ago. I've found my home.

And that, dear reader, is my wish for you as you make your way through this book and especially through the woods and fields. I hope that an awareness of birds and the experience of the fellowship of birders helps you find your home, too.

Beginning Birders

by Kenn Kaufman

A LONG, LONG TIME AGO—BACK IN THE 1980s—I SPENT the better part of five years researching writing, and illustrating a book that I called *A Field Guide to Advanced Birding*. When it was published in the Peterson Field Guide series in 1990, it drew a positive reception from serious birders, who appreciated its treatment of how to identify the most challenging birds.

Ten years and several book projects later, my *Kaufman Field Guide to Birds of North America* was published, and some of those same serious birders were openly critical and disappointed. The book wasn't what they had expected. I think they'd been hoping for something like *Even-More-Advanced Birding* or *Excruciatingly Extreme Birding*. What I had produced instead was a basic guide, designed to make the first step just as easy as possible for brand-new beginning birders.

So was this, as some of my friends suggested, a step backward? By making a transition from helping experts to helping beginners, did I become a traitor to serious birding?

I don't think so. I'm still fascinated by the minutiae of advanced bird ID and details of bird status and distribution. I still like to argue about obscure gulls and silent flycatchers. But as to where I should focus my work, I've concluded that for the future of birding and conservation, beginners are more important than experts.

Yes, more important.

In talking about beginning birders, a couple of misconceptions often come up. One is the idea that *beginners* automatically means *kids*. That's not necessarily true. Of course some beginners *are* kids, and of course kids are the key to the future. But a child or teenager who gets into birding often has the time and energy to learn very rapidly. Adults who start birding may have so many other commitments and distractions that it can take them much longer to learn the basics. So beginners who need help could be of any age. Trying to make things easier for beginners is not an insult to their intelligence—it's just a recognition of how hard it can be to get started.

Another error often made by experts is to assume that every newcomer is going to jump into birding in a serious way—that all beginners want to become experts themselves. I used to believe this myself, until countless conversations with new birders led me to a different conclusion. Yes, some love the challenge of building their skills, finding and identifying the toughest birds. But for others, birding is an escape, a chance to relax, and they really don't want it to be challenging.

In failing to recognize this, some experts—with the best of intentions—try to tell people how they "should" go birding. *You should memorize the official sequence of the checklist, even though it's likely to change again soon. You should go birding without your field guide, so you're forced to study and take notes on each bird. You should put down the camera and study the bird through binoculars.* But should you, in fact, heed such advice? That depends. If you've already decided to devote your whole life to bird study, then yes, you should probably do those things. If you just want to go birding for fun, you should do it however you like. As long as you're not doing harm to the birds or to other people, there is no "wrong" way to go birding.

This message is becoming more important, because there's now more interaction between seasoned experts and total beginners. At one time, most beginning birders were in their own backyards, while the most serious birders were checking out far-flung hot spots. That physical separation still holds—but now they meet constantly in cyberspace. On listservs and especially on social media, a person who has been birding for only a week may wind up communicating with someone who's been a birder for fifty years. The interactions don't always go well. When a newbie posts a photo of a female red-winged blackbird and asks "What kind of sparrow is this?" and when the same question has already been asked twenty times this week, experts in the group may get a little cranky.

And woe to the novice who goes online in May to report the "first robin of spring."

I went through a stage (when I'd been birding about fifteen years and thought I knew everything) when I was dismissive of beginners. But I've come around. Now I love going out with brand-new birders. They keep me grounded. They remind me of the magic of personal discovery. They remind me that the average person doesn't know words like *tertials* or *prealternate molt*. They remind me that many of our most common birds are stunningly gorgeous, and that we should gaze at them in awe whenever we get the chance.

Besides, as I said earlier, beginners are more important than experts—because there are more of them. The vast majority of birders will never become experts, and that's okay. Birds need all the friends they can get. Birds and their habitats face monumental threats today, and all the expert birders in the world don't add up to a large enough force to help them. We really don't need more people who can argue about the median coverts of Thayer's gulls, but we need millions more people who have maybe seen a yellow warbler and who understand that there's a connection between birds and their habitats. These are the people who provide the foundation for supporting bird conservation.

So better relations between experts and beginners would be good for all of us, including the birds. With that in mind, I have a couple of bits of advice:

1. If you're an expert birder and you're trying to remember how it felt when you were just getting started, tackle some area of natural history that you've never considered. Try identifying species of sedges, or ants, or lichens. Soon enough you'll be confused, and more sympathetic to beginners.

2. If you're relatively new to the field and someone is trying to tell you how you "should" approach birding, just smile and walk away. Birding is something we do for enjoyment, so if you enjoy it, you're a good birder. If you enjoy it a lot, you're a great birder. And as a great birder you shouldn't let anyone dampen your enthusiasm. I hope I'll see you out in the field!

KENN KAUFMAN burst onto the birding scene as a teenager in the 1970s, pursuing birds all over North America, as chronicled in his cult-classic book *Kingbird Highway*. After leading bird tours on all continents, he switched to a career as a writer and artist. He's now field editor for *Audubon* magazine and a Fellow of the American Ornithologists' Union, and has received the American Birding Association's lifetime achievement award twice.

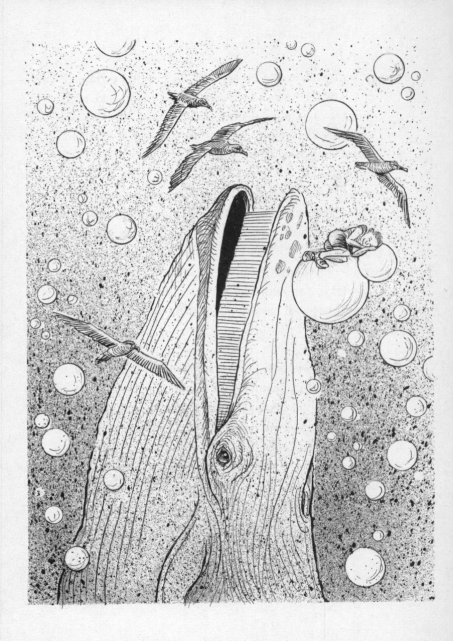

Go Birding with
(Young, *Really* Young) Children

by Ted Floyd

I STILL REMEMBER THE SONOGRAMS AND CHILDBIRTH classes. I can recall childproofing our home, and I haven't forgotten the solemn discussions about the baby's name. It's been a while, though, and those memories are starting to fade. But there's one memory I'll never let go of. I'll never forget a conversation with a birding friend, Virginia.

"Your kids are older now, Virginia, and they have their own interests and passions. But they're still into nature and the outdoors. How'd you do it? How'd you get them hooked on natural history?"

"Start early" was the entirety of her reply.

That's music to my ears, I thought. I started birding at the early age of twelve, and I know birders who started even younger—as early as first or second grade.

"How early?" I asked Virginia. "Kindergarten? Preschool?"

"Oh, that's too late," she said with a knowing laugh. "Go birding with them when they're infants, newborns even."

I pondered that for a moment and asked, "Really? Is it okay to do that? Is it safe? Is it effective? Is it *legal*?"

In an instant, we had moved on to some other topic of conversation—I don't remember what. But that remark by Virginia—"Go birding with them when they're infants, newborns even"—hit me like the proverbial ton of bricks. I knew I'd never forget it. I knew it was destined to change my life.

Is she serious? I guess so. I guess I'll give it a whirl.

A few months later, I got my chance. With my newborn daughter, just hours earlier released from the hospital, I went birding around the yard. A few months later, she and I were birding together in Tucson and then San Diego. Her first word—I swear, I'm not making this up—was the croak of a raven. (A raven called from a rooftop, and my daughter answered with an authentic, alveolar *cr-r-roak!*) And she finally got around to taking her first pelagic trip, out of Monterey, at the ripe old age of two.

Her younger brother, my son, also got off to a fast start. Within two hours of his birth, he and I were out on a hospital balcony, listening for great horned owls. In the ensuing months, he spent many a night out with me documenting a scientific phenomenon called nocturnal migration, but that's a story for another time. The story I want to tell now is the story of my son's first pelagic trip.

It was the same basic deal as with his sister: aboard the *Princess Monterey,* we searched for black-footed albatrosses and sooty shearwaters. We saw two of the former and a hundred of the latter, and my son was well pleased. Then he did something perfectly normal. He did something I've seen from umpteen birders on umpteen pelagic trips: having gotten his birds, he fell asleep.

Next thing you know, a blue whale, on anybody's short list of the greatest animals in the history of life on Earth, sidled up to the *Princess*. People were crying. A woman played panpipes. Someone else was in an apparent trance. This was so powerful, so real, that, for once in this digital era of ours, people just stood there in awe and wonder. No cameras, no smartphones, just smiles and tears.

It got better. The whale, literally close enough to touch, let out a mighty blow. We laughed and cried as we were drizzled in water, gas, and mucus.

Meanwhile, my son—remember him?—was sound asleep. Not in the galley, but at the far end of the stern, right up against the railing, right next to the whale. He'd simply rolled over to that position, and there he was, sleeping soundly in a thin blanket of whale mucus.

"Don't you want to wake him up?" a passenger asked me. "This is a once-in-a-lifetime experience. He'll never forget it."

He probably *wouldn't* remember it, I reasoned. He was awfully young. Besides, he was *sleeping,* for crying out loud, and the cardinal rule of parenting—I didn't need Virginia to tell me this one—is never to wake a sleeping baby.

But I had another concern, another preoccupation. The whole time I was watching my sleeping son (admittedly, with greater nervousness than I let on to the other passengers), I couldn't help but think about something else. It's something I've been reflecting on ever since. It's become a worldview, a way of life; and that is the matter to which I now turn.

I hope my two children—on the verge now of becoming teenagers—have enjoyed all the birding and nature study they've done with me. I hope they've learned some science and environmentalism along the way. And I hope they'll apply all those experiences in ways that make a difference in this world we all share. But that's *their* story, and it would be presumptuous of me to try to tell it.

Forgive me if this comes across the wrong way, but all those birding excursions with my young children have brought satisfaction and immeasurable joy to *me*. Oh, sure, there were some annoyances along the way: it's hard to ID a sandpiper when you're changing a diaper. And there were some scary moments: please don't remind me about the time my daughter bounced off the dam breast, or the time my son reached into the cactus for a cool insect.

But check this out: those various experiences, and thousands more like them, got me out birding. I've actually done more birding, *much* more birding, since my kids were born. Young children have to be dealt with *right now*. You can't delay or procrastinate, as you can with such adult concerns as deadlines, personal hygiene, and paying the bills. Parenting can't wait. And I've elected to do as much of it as possible while birding.

A little while ago, I met up with Virginia at lunch on a Christmas Bird Count. It was a family affair: she was there with her husband, her brother-in-law, and one of her adult children. My kids were there, too, accompanied by two of their teenage friends. This was no local, casual, walk-in-the-park affair. Don't tell the truant officer, but it was a school day, and we were a hundred miles from home. We'd driven down overnight, and we'd had a wonderfully exhausting morning.

I'll say it again: I hope my two children had a good time. And I'll say this again: I know *I* had a good time, a glorious time, that morning.

I wouldn't have done it without my kids. I couldn't have justified the time away from work—or from my spouse (that would be my kids' mother), who deserves a shout-out here. And I reflect on an almost daily basis, on the wisdom of Virginia: Just do it. Start early. Pack the diaper kit. Go birding.

TIPS

- Just do it.
- Start early.
- Pack the diaper kit.
- Go birding.

▸▹•◂◂

TED FLOYD is the editor of *Birding* magazine, published by the American Birding Association. He is the author of four books and more than two hundred popular articles and scientific papers on birds and nature. Ted has served on the boards of several nonprofit ornithological societies, and he is a frequent speaker at bird club meetings and birding festivals. He and his family live in Boulder County, Colorado.

Summer of the Sparrow

by Lili Taylor

I FOUND A PLACE IN RURAL UPSTATE NEW YORK FIFTEEN years ago. The land was bucolic, a pastoral paradise. A cartoon fairy tale with melodious bird song and playful birds flittering to and fro. The sweetness lasted until last summer, and then the true essence of the fairy tale broke through: that moment when the maiden must enter the forest to witness the darkness firsthand. *I* entered that proverbial forest to fight a brutal war with a male house sparrow. I bought a pellet gun, devised a death chamber, and arranged an execution. But the story begins with two bluebirds.

Right after I moved upstate I started monitoring bluebird nest boxes. I had very few problems save for some pesky blowflies and one rained-out nest. Last summer that all changed when a male house sparrow showed up. My neighbor had started raising chickens, and I think the cheap grain brought the sparrows in.

I had three bluebird boxes up at the time. One box held a

pair who had just completed nest building. Another had five healthy chicks, and the third was empty—or so I thought.

It was June and still. The mating frenzy had lulled into concentrated incubation and diligent feeding.

I was making my rounds monitoring the boxes. I tapped lightly on the nest box with the chicks. Usually after the tap they flutter in place, squeaking, yellow mouths open wide. It was too quiet. I lifted the door and craned my neck to see inside.

Five baby bluebirds lay in a lifeless heap, massacred.

I touched their bodies to feel for warmth, breath. None. I lifted the nest out with purpose but had no clue what to do. I brought the lifeless nest to the bench, then went to the second nest box and, with dread, lifted the door.

A female bluebird lay dead on the nest with her eyes gouged out.

I looked over at the third nest box. On top of it perched a lone house sparrow, chirping relentlessly—a sound I later learned is called the "chirp of death." I walked toward him, but he flew away. Not too far but just far enough so I couldn't grab him. I opened up the nest box. Inside was a messy, disorganized nest, like some careless slob had made it. And inside this hodgepodge of natural material were two eggs.

I went inside and entered the world of *Passer domesticus* through the bluebird website sialis.org. This quote begins the over twenty-page-long chapter on the house sparrow: "Without question the most deplorable event in the history of American ornithology was the introduction of the English Sparrow." (W. L. Dawson, *The Birds of Ohio,* 1903)

And then I found this: "I pray that you never have to experience the shock of opening a nest box to find a nest full of babies, mutilated and dying, or on the ground, covered with ants, or broken eggs, or a blood-covered mother bluebird who fatally tried to protect her young."

There are passive and aggressive ways to deal with the house sparrow. The author asks that you be clear where you stand: if passive means don't work and you can't go nuclear, then you shouldn't have bluebird boxes at all.

Some important things I learned:

• The house sparrow claims a nest site over a mate and can claim many boxes, even though it won't use them.
• It is pointless to remove the nest. They will just keep rebuilding. Plus, removing the nest has been known to incite the sparrow to go on a rampage in that they become severely agitated and start looking at other cavities nearby and begin destroying all eggs as well as unfeathered young.
• There are ways of dealing with the sparrow eggs. One way is to boil them.

I ladled the eggs into the boiling water with the care used for something precious. I was jacked up the way you are after five cups of coffee, yet I was careful and precise. My thinking became focused and obsessed. If someone had tried to talk

to me about something else at that moment I wouldn't have heard a thing. I had only one thing on my mind. I more or less stayed in that state for the next two months.

As covertly as possible, I returned the well-done eggs to the nest. The female entered the box to incubate. I knew she was sitting on a pair of duds and I didn't feel bad at all. In fact, I felt good because I was winning.

For two days I patiently waited. I'd sit outside and nonchalantly look over at the sparrow box, confident she would give up at some point and abandon the nest. The childless pair of bluebirds were ready to get going on the next clutch. The widowed male bluebird was singing his soft song and investigating the newly cleaned nest box. The sparrow darted back and forth between the nest boxes, snuffing out any attempt at life making.

What was taking her so long? My giddiness shifted into agitation. I waited for her to fly out for her daily meal. I opened the door to the box.

One of the boiled eggs had hatched!

And as I named him The Terminator I thought of Maleficent in *Sleeping Beauty,* "before the sun sets on your sixteenth birthday . . ."

In the meantime I had to take down either the father or the nest boxes.

It is legal to kill a house sparrow.

I bought a pellet gun and watched YouTube videos on

how to shoot. I set up a low-to-the-ground hunting chair and staked out the father. I kept missing. A hunter told me it's nearly impossible to shoot at a distance with a pellet gun. I put the gun away.

I jerry-rigged a trapdoor over the entrance hole. A long kite string led from the flimsy trapdoor to my hand. I waited. It fell. I re-rigged. He went in, I pulled too hard. The door fell off, he flew out.

I got a special trapdoor specifically made to trap sparrows. I trapped the male bluebird instead. Thankfully, he wasn't trapped for long.

I set up a trap similar to a Havahart trap but designed for birds. A song sparrow got trapped and died.

I hated that father sparrow. It was strange to feel such strong feelings about a bird, something that had no idea that I thought about him, looked for him, waited for him, plotted against him, was frustrated by him, was obsessed with him.

I sat vigil on that hunting chair like an edgy soldier. I was distracted when friends came by, looked out the corner of my eye when I was playing with kids. Nobody else knew the life-and-death drama that was playing out right next to us. I knew because I was tuned in to every noise, movement, struggle. If you penetrate into the natural world and stay, the wealth of data is enormous. It was as if a highly sensitive microphone was picking up and heightening every call, alarm, sound, distress, fear. Things happened fast and moved quickly. I could look away for a second and miss the spar and parry, and by the time I looked back some bird would be hurt or dead.

The Terminator had grown. Father and son were now a team.

My neighbor Mike, a solid man in his eighties, shoots clay pigeons. He has lived in the country all his life and understands its rhythms. I asked him if he would shoot the father and son sparrows. He nodded and got his gun.

The father sparrow was perched on the bluebird nest box. Mike blew him away with one shot. It made Mike feel useful, and it was the first relief I'd felt in a month.

Now for the son.

But the son had been watching us. He was hiding. He'd witnessed the death of his father and was gun-shy. We gave it a break, then tried some more, to no avail. Mike couldn't get him.

I took down all the nest boxes. The widowed male bluebird continued to sing until the end of summer, even though it was far too late to mate. The trees' leaves fell, and the male drifted away.

This February I saw a male and female bluebird. They might have been offspring from a previous brood of last year's childless pair. I'm not sure.

Later I talked to some of the kids who were up at the house last summer. They asked if the sparrow was still here. Asked if I could open the nest box so they could hold a baby bluebird. Last summer they held baby bluebirds in their little hands. They checked them for blowflies. They had the privilege to bear witness to a life-and-death struggle play out in the natural world before their very eyes. What could I tell them?

"I've given up. Yup. It's all too much. The sparrow won. Bluebirds lost."

Is that who I want to be?

I found a sparrow-resistant nest box made out of PVC pipe, designed by someone who also didn't surrender. It's called the Gilbertson nest box. The kids helped me put it up.

TIPS
- If I were to do it all over again I would first visit www .sialis.org and read their advice for new bluebirders.
- I would follow their eight steps to take for a successful monitoring experience.
- If bluebird monitoring proves to be too difficult, you can always get some mealworms at a bird supply store and put them out for the bluebirds to enjoy—and for you to enjoy watching them.

L ILI TAYLOR has worked in theater, film, and television for the past thirty years. Most recently she can be seen in the award-winning TV show *American Crime.* She proudly serves on the board of the American Birding Association and the National Audubon Society.

Chasing Jaegers
How Taking New Shots at Local Patch Birding Can Reach a Boatload of People

by Jen Brumfield

O NE OF THE MOST FASCINATING AND STUNNING ASPECTS of birding is its profound ability to pull on the heartstrings of countless diverse peoples around the world. We all see birds—even if they go unidentified and unrecognized as to their full splendor, stories, and natural history. We all see birds. Their capability of flight and lavish array of colors and sounds combine to render each of us awestruck or, at the very least, fascinated and momentarily captivated or charmed at even a glimpse.

Connecting people to birds enlightens ones place and space on this planet and cultivates a connection, meaning, and discovery. The stories of how these sometimes random, sometimes peculiar, often ironic and delightful connections spark, evolve, and grow impassioned should not be whispered. They should be shouted. They should be loud.

Very loud.

I cleared my throat. Coughed out a bit of excitement and nervousness.

This could be it.

Had another sip of coffee. Dialed the number and waited.

"HULLO, Fisherman's Wharf, TIM SPEAKING."

He shouted that. He shouted that into the phone. Perfectly gruff and rough.

"Hi there, good morning. I have some questions about your charters. I'm hoping to talk to the captain to see if I can run a special kind of boat trip."

"WELL THAT'S ME."

"Great, I'm looking to do some birding trips out on the la—"

Interrupted. "BIRDERS . . . HOLD ON."

Rustling. Dull shout overheard: "Hey Jimmy, BIRD watchers want the BOAT." *He tried to muffle it with his shoulder or hand.*

More rustling.

He's back.

"OK. WE'VE GOT BIRDS. WE'VE GOT CORMORANTS AND EAGLES AND HERONS. You want me to take you up the river? We've had them cormorants by the hundreds right from shore. AND THE WHITE EGRETS. THE BIG ONES. And the seagulls with the BLACK BACKS."

Still shouting. I like this guy.

"Awesome. Those birds are great. They're really great. Black-backed gulls. That's fantastic. We're looking for some birds that are out on the middle of the lake. Ten miles, twenty miles out."

Long pause.

"WHAT THE HELL ARE YOU GONNA SEE OUT THERE. WE ONLY SEE SEAGULLS OUT THERE."

The challenge. I started to chug my coffee.

"That. Exactly that. We want those seagulls We want rare seagulls. And birds called jaegers that chase them d—"

"JAEGER?"

"—down. Jaegers are sort of like falcons but they're seabirds. They're offshore. What we'd need is . . . if we saw a special gull or a jaeger . . . we'd need you to drive the boat really fast. Fast. To chase that jaeger. To stay with it and put it on either side of the boat for folks to see."

Complete silence.

Processing.

More silence.

Then it clicked: A bird that sounds like liquor. Driving fast. Canadian border.

"I CAN DRIVE THAT BOAT FAST."

Yes. You. Can.

"Absolutely. I'm in. We're pumped."

"WELL THE WAVES GET BIG. THEY CAN GET

BIG OUT THERE. AND IT'S COLD. WIND'LL PICK UP THEM WAVES IN AN INSTANT. YOU MIGHT GET SICK."

"That's great. Majority of the folks that come will have been on boats before. On the ocean."

Silence.

"YOU SURE YOU DON'T WANT TO SEE THEM PRETTY WHITE EGRETS, THEY'RE RIGHT ALONG THE SHORE."

"That sounds fun too. Maybe we could do that sometime. We're excited to get out there on the lake. It'll be awesome."

"WELP. OK. I'LL TAKE YOU OUT THERE. I'LL SHOW YOU YOUR SEAGULLS."

"Rock on, man."

"WHAT DAY ARE YOU LOOKING AT."

"We want to do five or six trips."

Silence.

"OK. HERE WE GO. GIMME A SECOND. LET ME GET MY BOOK." *Rustling.* "JIMMY, the BIRD watchers want the boat five times."

I heard that.

"ALRIGHT. GOT MY BOOK. WHEN."

"September. October. November."

We arrive at the docks in a mass cluster of vibrating joy and humming excitement. The group has dressed for hurricane conditions even though Lake Erie has a mere two- to three-foot chop this fine morning. Some are in full waterproof camo. Others look like SWAT. Ready for the first full day's "pelagic" on Lake Erie. The first of its kind in Ohio, an organized opportunity to be consistently ten to twenty miles offshore and cover seventy or more miles of open water. Conditions: excellent. Timing: well within the windows of opportunity for Sabine's gull and long-tailed and parasitic jaeger. Chum ready. Boots on. Bins up.

A beast of a black truck rolls up behind the group. Two doors slam and Tim and his first mate stroll over to the trip briefing.

Tim takes a few looks around the group.

And promptly starts shouting.

"BIRD WATCHERS. I THOUGHT YOU'D SHOW UP IN YOUR SHORTS."

Pause.

"YOU DRESS BETTER THAN HALF THE FISHERMEN COME ON MY CHARTERS, I'LL GIVE YA THAT."

"Folks! Tim, our capta—"

Interrupted, deliciously.

"WE'RE GONNA HAVE A GREAT TIME. WE'RE GONNA GET OUT THERE AND GET YOU SOME BIRDS. WHAT WE'RE LOOKING FOR TODAY IS JAEGERS. AND RARE SEAGULLS."

Naw—no he didn't. He did not just say that. Yes he did.

A full safety announcement, key boating terms, introduction of the guides, final comments, and the engine's on. Everybody settles in and checks cameras, cleans binoculars.

"Tim, this is great. Awesome to meet you. We're stoked."

"YOU BIRDERS. I THOUGHT YOU'D BE IN YOUR SHORTS."

He's stuck on that.

"We're ready. Okay! So. This is how this thing goes. If I spot a jaeger, I'm going to yell to you. Rush up to you, to point in the direction of the bird. And I'll keep communicating to you, constantly, where the bird is, so you know where to go. Just go fast. They're fast. We may have to cut hard to the left or right. Or pull a full one-eighty."

"OHHKAYY. I BET WE GET A BLACK BACK GULL."

"Yes. Let's do that."

Common and Forster's terns. A tight flock of black terns. Tim's great black-backed gulls. Lesser black-backed gull. Bonaparte's gulls.

Flocks of Bonaparte's gulls. No seagulls so far.

We're eight miles offshore and pushing, and zipping around flocks of Bonaparte's gulls.

Tim gets on the radio.

"YEP. I'VE GOT THE BIRD WATCHERS. WE'RE LOOKING AT THE GULLS. WHAT? NO. NOT THE JAEGERS YET."

My god. His crew on the other side of the radio are asking about the jaegers.

Then it happens. We're relentlessly scanning the horizon and poring through flocks of terns and Bonaparte's gulls, and then it happens. We knew it would.

I scream. "Jaeger jaeger jaeger two o'clock! Jaeger two o'clock. Parasitic jaeger. Chasing Bonie. TIIIIIIIMMMMMM!"

Like Secretariat on the last leg of the world-shocking run, Tim connects. It's slow motion, but it's so fast. I point and scream. Tim peers over his shoulder, sees me wide-eyed. He looks back out onto the lake. The wheel of the boat spins hard to the right.

"OOOOOHHHHHHHKAAAAAAYYYYYYYYY."

He looks fierce.

"GIVE IT ALL YOU'VE GOT, MAN." (*Now* I'm *yelling. We're yelling. We're all yelling.*)

Then something I've never seen before. Through a nicked and spray-coated window, Tim squints and—*finds the jaeger.* It's a spot. A dark spot.

"I'VE GOT IT. I'VE GOT THE THING."

My god, yes, he does.

"PUT IT ON THE RIGHT, TIM, ON THE RIGHT. YOU'VE GOT THIS. IT'S STILL AT TWO O'CLOCK."

He puts it on the right. Full parallel. For ten minutes he

cuts the chop and weaves and double-backs and puts it back on the right each time.

Stunning views of parasitic jaeger, eleven miles offshore. And another, later that day, fourteen miles offshore.

Gulls, terns, migrant shorebirds, waterfowl—birds that would never have been documented, for the record, otherwise. A new world of birding. A new effort for Ohio birding.

We're nearly back to shore when the radio buzzes.

"YEP. NOPE. YEP. YEP, WE GOT THE JAEGERS. YEP, WE'VE GOT FIVE MORE OF THESE TRIPS. WE'RE GONNA GET 'EM. WE'RE GONNA GET EVERYTHING OUT HERE."

Yes. We. Are.

TIPS

- As birding continues to swell in popularity and as big years, big days, big sits, and big hours gain more and more attention, and prime birding hot spots around the world garner even larger visitation, it could appear that new opportunities within the hobby have all been spoken for. This couldn't be further from the birding truth. Bird your local patch. There are new discoveries to be made each month, each season, and each year even in your own city or county. Visit new sites that lack any or current eBird checklists and submit new data. Get out and be the one who answers the questions that still remain about migration patterns and appearances, routes, and so much more. Whether you boat, bike, run, walk, or skip your way to a new place, even if it's just around the corner, there are endless new experiences and observations that await.

- Share your zest. Not everyone will dive passionately into birding or embrace it with massive joy and huge fascination. But even a brief glimpse into the birding world may just be enough to tip the scales toward their choosing to support conservation causes and respect for the natural world.

J EN BRUMFIELD eagerly combines her passions for extreme birding, field studies, outdoor education, and detailed scientific illustration into a truly "wild" career. Each year, Jen reaches thousands of children through outdoor education programming as a naturalist with Cleveland Metroparks. She has authored and illustrated seven natural history field guides, and is an active rep with Leica's Birding Optics Pro Staff team. Currently residing in Cleveland, Ohio, she runs multiple "pelagic" boat trips on Lake Erie each fall and is forever scouring the lakefront for birds rare to the county.

New York City Birding
Is the Best Birding

by Corey Finger

THE EXACT MOMENT WHEN I REALIZED THAT I LIVE IN the best place in the world to be a birder is unclear to me. It might have been when I watched a prothonotary warbler hop between a homeless man's feet at Bryant Park. It could have been while watching the first Couch's kingbird ever seen in New York State catching bugs from fire escapes in the West Village. Perhaps it was when I saw a Bicknell's thrush singing in Forest Park, a Connecticut warbler wandering on the lawn in Madison Square Park, or the second record of gray-hooded gull in North America feeding on French fries at Coney Island. To paraphrase a rather famous line about New York City, if you can bird here, you can bird anywhere.

Back in 2008 I left the comfort of my natal home in upstate New York and moved to Queens, the finest of New York City's five boroughs. I did so for love, of course, but not for love of birds, though I did hold out for an apartment close enough to Forest Park that I could easily walk there. And it's a

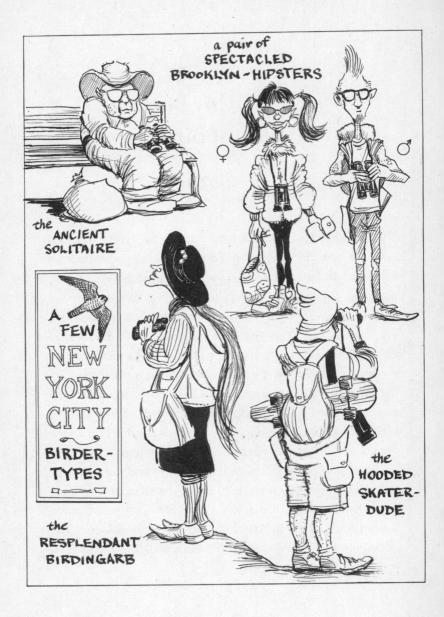

a pair of
SPECTACLED
BROOKLYN - HIPSTERS

the
ANCIENT
SOLITAIRE

A
FEW
NEW
YORK
CITY
BIRDER-
TYPES

the
RESPLENDANT
BIRDINGARB

the
HOODED
SKATER-
DUDE

good thing I insisted on that apartment, because for the first three years I lived in Gotham, I did so without the benefit of an automobile, which meant that to see birds I had to get to them on foot, by mass transit, or by bumming rides.

The lack of a car would turn out not to be much of a hindrance, as the mass transit system in New York City is simply amazing. From Van Cortlandt Park way up in the Bronx to the parks along Staten Island's eastern shore, from the heart of the city in Bryant Park to the beaches in the Rockaways, you can get there by mass transit. Sure, it often meant getting up absurdly early and deflecting questioning looks from bleary-eyed club kids heading home while I lugged a scope on the subway, but it was totally worth it! I don't think any other city in the United States has as many varied habitats reachable by mass transit.

And the birders! What networks of birders we have in New York City! There are the Brooklyn birders who peer into every portion of Prospect Park and take pride in their ability to find plenty of rarities along the coast. The Central Park birding scene can be absolutely insane, with the Christmas Bird Count covering every single inch of the park and a nice May day bringing hundreds into the Ramble to look for Neotropical migrants. Staten Island, always suffering from an inferiority complex, remains insular, and word of good birds there often takes time to get out, but they find some amazing species across their suburban borough. The Bronx, with its rich ornithological history, has perhaps the smallest number of birders at this point, but they do have Roger Tory Peterson, who started work on his eponymous field guide while living there, and they are proud of their sightings at Pelham Bay Park and the New York City Botanical Gardens. Of course Queens, where I found myself, has a pretty impressive bunch of birders as well, from a savant who can identify chip notes from a mile away to the aficionados of the waterhole where catching a twenty-warbler morning from the comfort of a lawn chair lugged into the woods is a matter of course at the peak of spring migration.

The best part about New York City's birders is how willing everyone is to help you find your way around and see birds. Within weeks of my having moved to Queens, I had been offered rides to chase after rarities, been given informal walking tours through several parks to show me the good spots, and been invited to join several different bird organizations, of which we have a plethora. We have the New York City Audubon Society, the Queens County Bird Club, the Brooklyn Bird Club, and the Linnaean Society of New York. And you can forget neither that the National Audubon Society is headquartered in New York, nor the wonderful resources at the American Museum of Natural History and the Wildlife Conservation Society's zoos in each borough. Perhaps as important as any of the clubs is the presence of the Strand, the best used bookstore I have ever visited, with an impressive and ever-changing selection of field guides, natural history books, and other volumes to keep a birder entertained and educated.

Besides the sheer number of birders, amazing birding locations, and birding resources, there is another thing that makes New York City the best birding spot—the most important thing. And that thing is, of course, the multitude of birds that migrate through the city. The level of development in and around the New York City metropolitan area is huge, which means that birds have fewer spots to rest and refuel. Even the smallest green spots can be loaded with birds on days with heavy migration. Who can resist lots of birds in a small area?

The combination of lots of birders, lots of birds, and our modern communication technology allows for word of rarities to spread frequently and with blinding speed. In the spring it is not unusual for crowds of birders to wander from a hooded warbler to a cerulean warbler in Central Park as news of the birds spreads through Facebook, Twitter, text message, email listservs, and good old-fashioned word-of-mouth. The problem in such situations isn't finding the location where the bird is, but finding a way to get a look at it through the gaps between other birders' heads and binoculars.

Lest solitary birders shudder at the thought of being forced to bird with the unwashed hordes (and, trust me, when migration is hopping, some dedicated birders forget to eat, much less bathe), there are still plenty of places in New York City where you can spend the whole day birding and not run into another birder. The vast expanses of Pelham Bay Park, the barrier beaches in Queens, and a whole host of other locations are relatively under-birded. Getting out and exploring spots that most birders don't go is rewarding in and of itself, though if you find something really good and get the word out, you can expect to give up your solitude pretty quickly.

Whether you come to New York on a day trip, because of a long layover at one of our airports, or on a family vacation, you can have a great birding outing. Even if you are traveling with nonbirders, they are going to want to see Central Park, visit Prospect Park, or take a ride on the Staten Island Ferry, all activities that will have you seeing birds. Even the top of the Empire State Building can provide great birding once the sun goes down and nocturnal migrants start streaming past. Come to New York City, tell 'em I sent you, and see why New York is the center of the (birding) world.

TIPS for Birding in New York City
- Mass transit is a quick and cheap way to get around the city.
- There are many kind and helpful birders in New York City who will help you find birds.
- Birding in the smallest of parks can be rewarding because birds can show up anywhere.

>▷•◁<

COREY FINGER is a proud Queens birder who is happiest when he is seeing a life bird in his home borough. He is co-owner and managing editor of *10,000 Birds,* the world's most-read bird blog, and the author of the *American Birding Association Field Guide to Birds of New York*. His bird photographs have appeared in a wide variety of outlets, including the television show *Today,* as well as *Birding* and *Bird Watcher's Digest* magazines.

Doorknobs, Bird Songs, and Remembering Where You Put Your Car Keys

by Tom Stephenson

A NUMBER OF YEARS BACK I MADE A STUDY OF DOORKNOBS. More accurately, doorknobs, doors, gates, windows, and other such architectural features. Traveling for work, I found myself walking through a range of new and old neighborhoods across the United States. The variety and abundance of details (along with my lack of knowledge) created a sensory blur that was a barrier to appreciation. Focusing on one aspect of these man-made environments created an entry point for a deeper appreciation of the design histories and the aesthetic decisions made by the builders. Instead of a bland blur, focusing on even these few architectural details helped me begin to notice differences in styles: Victorian, Neoclassical, Italianate, and more. Even a little knowledge offered me a path to a richer experience and greater appreciation of my urban surroundings.

I know a number of people who, when walking through a park or woodland, experience that same kind of pleasant yet vague, almost opaque, experience of the sounds and sights around them; a world too remote or unknown to provide any exciting details. For me, birds and, especially, bird vocalizations are the doors into that natural world. And just as a modest study of architectural detail creates a path for our senses—or better, gives us an excuse to be more observant—listening to bird song reveals a world populated with detail and richness as one observation leads to the next and to many more.

The very good news is that it doesn't take much study to trick our minds into paying more attention to something. Once even a few songs have been learned, walking through a park becomes an exciting rendezvous with old friends and unexpected exotic visitors. Even a minimal framework provides reference points that we can then use for comparison and new learning. Eventually, a three-dimensional world is revealed, populated by an incredibly varied, rich, and ever-changing cohort of creatures announcing their presence, competing for mates and territories, and sounding alarms.

Overhead a blue jay mimics a red-tailed hawk, trying to scare a flock away from their food. A distant tufted titmouse starts proclaiming its home turf only to be answered immediately by a rival neighbor. A pine warbler trills from a nearby treetop, feeling its hormones. A magnolia warbler sings lower down in a nearby yew and is soon joined by the *chip*s of two or three yellow-rumped warblers partaking in the feeding frenzy created by an insect bloom. In some dense understory a harsh, flat *chip* reveals a common yellowthroat. A downy woodpecker whinnies and proclaims its territory with unexpectedly loud tapping, having found the most resonant branch in its area. A sudden silencing of all voices is followed by the authentic call of a real red-tailed hawk, maybe annoyed at the blue jay's weaker imitation.

It does take some work to go beyond those familiar species, like northern cardinal, American robin, or yellow warbler, that we've heard so many times. Learning vocalizations is a difficult challenge for most of us. We just don't hear many species often enough in the field to have them deeply etched into our memories. And even hours of listening to a CD doesn't yield very long-term benefits. Are there any methods or tricks that might help, that might make learning more efficient and thereby enrich our listening experiences?

Years ago I began to travel to see birds in exotic lands around the world. For these trips I wanted to replicate the feeling of familiarity I had on my home turf. This required learning many, often hundreds of vocalizations for bird-rich countries—a very daunting task. Failing many times, I finally decided that I had to study memory theory to find out how to efficiently learn something as abstract as songs. As might be expected, how we humans (and many other species) learn has been heavily studied for years. And although there's still much to be uncovered, there are core techniques that have been confirmed effective by many diverse studies. Using this information, I eventually was able to learn many vocalizations for my overseas journeys. The good news is that the effective techniques are very simple. And it takes a surprisingly small amount of time to learn fifty or a hundred vocalizations using just a few basic strategies. I've listed the main methods I use in the tips below.

Listening to and studying all of those songs brought to light another important problem with vocalizations. We have lots of terminology to describe species. Birders know and have studied wing bars, eye lines, undertails, and many other specific areas of bird anatomy. This terminology acts as a set of pointers, helping us focus on key ID characteristics that we might have missed otherwise. It also provides a language that helps us communicate what we're seeing.

No such system exists for bird song. *Tseet seet* doesn't really cut it when you're trying to learn the unique characteristics of a vocalization. And these subjective transliterations are also useless when trying to communicate or remember what you've heard. Struggling with this problem, I, with Scott Whittle, eventually created a simple, objective system that can be used to describe and compare vocalizations. Even a few simple, structural characteristics of a song, when noticed, can help us learn, compare, and remember even complex vocalizations. Some of the results of that study made their way into *The Warbler Guide,* which provides a simple language to describe the unique, memorable, objective characteristics of each species' vocalizations. This strategy also resulted in the creation of the book's song finders, which aid in identifying an unknown song: simple objective questions like how many times an element or phrase is repeated, and how many sections, or obvious changes in speed, pitch, or quality, occur in one song.

Of course, feeling an almost gravitational pull from bird vocalizations can have its benefits. One time I was in downtown Nashville with some nonbirding colleagues. It was starting to get dark and everyone was weighing in on where we should go for dinner. Suddenly I said, "Do you hear that?" Blank stares. "There . . ."

No response; but now people were listening hard.

"There . . . listen for a short *peent* . . ."

Then one by one they all realized they really had heard the sound. Shortly thereafter, a common nighthawk flew lower into a streetlight, calling to the now appreciative group. The general reaction was: "How did you ever hear that in all of this traffic?" And from then on I was the guy with the super-hearing. (Not true—I've got my share of rock-induced tinnitus—but the reputation did curtail the odd gossiping when I was nearby.)

I'm always eager to introduce anyone I can to the songs around them. I once visited a friend living on Long Island in a home with a small backyard. She loved birds and had a feeder set up near her flower garden. I asked her what birds she had in her yard. Not being an avid birder, she knew she had a cardinal and a robin and some kind of woodpecker, but that was about it. When I visited her one summer I heard twelve species vocalizing. I pointed out house wren, three species of woodpeckers, American goldfinch, song sparrow, red-eyed vireo, and others. Very excited, she got some binocs and started down the path to becoming a birder.

So for me, a love of bird songs has opened many doors. Careful listening provides a clear, three-dimensional map of all of the songsters around me and helps me find birds I really want to see during spring and fall migration. Pre-trip song memorization greatly enriches my enjoyment when I have a chance to go birding in places I've never before visited. Most importantly, paying attention to every sound I hear draws me more deeply into, and gives me greater pleasure in and appreciation for, even the most familiar landscapes.

And yes, using basic memory theory to learn these vocalizations in the first place has the added benefit of helping you remember where you put your car keys!

TIPS: What Memory Theory Tells Us about How to Learn More Songs

- Start with only four or five songs.
- Listen to each a few times with your eyes closed and see what images you conjure for each song. For a black-and-white warbler it might be a squeaky bike wheel. For a yellow warbler it might be *sweet sweet sweet I'm so sweet.*
- Find a way of connecting that image to the name of the bird. This is a critical step and becomes easier and easier the more it's practiced. The squeaky-wheeled bike might be driven by a masked thief wearing black-and-white striped prison garb. The warbler that is so sweet might be covered in honey, making it yellow all over.
- Wait just a couple of minutes.
- Test yourself on these few songs, making sure you can't see or hear the song name. Re-create the image, connect the name, and then check. This almost-immediate testing, using active recall, is the crucial key to success.
- Review these few songs another couple of times during the day.
- Once you learn them (you will be amazed at how fast you do learn them), go on to another small group.
- Every couple of days review, using active recall, the songs you've already learned.

That's it. Good luck; it's worth it!

Tᴏᴍ Sᴛᴇᴘʜᴇɴsᴏɴ is coauthor, with Scott Whittle, of the award-winning *The Warbler Guide* book and app. His latest project is the BirdGenie app, which will help users identify singing birds. His articles and photographs are in museums and many publications. His team holds the U.S. Big Day Photo record. As a musician, he worked with several Grammy and Academy Award winners and retired as director of technology at Roland Corporation.

County by County

The Joys of Being an Unrepentant, and Utterly Pedantic, Lister

by Nate Swick

THERE'S A PATCH OF ORGANIC FARMLAND IN THE FAR northeast corner of Guilford County, North Carolina, where I go sometimes when I need to see some open-country birds. It's the one place I know I can be sure to see bobolinks every May, dozens of the squirrely patchwork blackbirds singing their stitched-together song as they pick up and drop down into the verdant rows of soybeans. I've seen dickcissel there too, and white-crowned sparrow and the first sedge wrens in Guilford County in more than twenty years. And it's a place I wouldn't ever see if I didn't care deeply about finding birds in this square patch of Piedmont in North Carolina. Just two hundred meters down the road is Alamance County, an entirely different playing field for another day, but today it might as well be China. I'm a county lister, and I'm proud of it.

I know that keeping lists gets a bad rap sometimes. There's a certain obsessiveness to it that cannot be denied. To be a *lister* is to turn birds into commodities or, worse, mere numbers devoid of meaning. The word practically invites you to sneer when you say it. And to be a county lister? To break the already arbitrary political boundaries of the United States into their most arbitrary segments? It's inane. It's fanatical. It's birding pedantry at its most pedantic. And it's glorious.

I certainly don't buy the argument that keeping lists is an impediment to the sort of aesthetic satisfaction that comes from watching birds. Lists are many things to many people. They can be totems, for sure, or they can be aspirational. For most of us, they're logged memories of experiences, incredible places enjoyed with wonderful people. The competitive aspect is undeniable, but it's typically a good-natured, rising-tide-lifts-all-boats sort of thing. At our best, we share knowledge freely in order to share these experiences. So I'm all for keeping a list, in whatever way is meaningful to the birder. If it manifests itself in an attempt to count birds in your yard, or your state, or the six hundred or so square miles surrounding your hometown, who am I to judge? If a list encourages you to go out and find birds, it's a good thing.

And finding birds is an incredible and wonderful challenge. It requires skill, to be sure, not only to know what you're looking at when you find it, but to know the best places to focus your attention. If we think of birding as a treasure hunt, then the map of North America has been long since established, published in dozens of field guides at your fingertips.

That treasure is so completely excavated that any searcher can find it more or less at their leisure. But shrink the parameters of that map a bit, and the treasure becomes a little harder to find. Shrink it even more and suddenly there are untold riches still buried all around you, waiting for someone to dig them up. This is county birding at its core. The political boundaries are arbitrary, but the birds aren't.

Being conscious of county lines when you are birding opens up a whole new aspect of bird finding. Sure, there's the game involved—trying to find new birds in each county is fun—but, as in all things birding, it is in service to something bigger. You might know the muddy ditches for Wilson's snipe near your home, but what about in the next county over? And the next one beyond that? What kind of habitat are you looking for when you're looking for Wilson's snipe? Suddenly, instead of associating Wilson's snipe with a particular place, you're associating it with a *type* of place. You're more aware of the habitat requirements of snipe, and maybe the northern harrier and the American pipits you saw there, too. Now you can go to these sorts of places in other counties and find these birds. Yeah, you can add them to your list, and that's undeniably fun, but more than growing a list, you're growing knowledge. For birders, knowledge is a far more valuable currency than ticks on a list. This is true even if it consists of a mental map of Walmart parking lots where house sparrows can be found.

And at a personal level, there's something even more valuable that comes from paying attention to county lines. It's incredibly satisfying to deeply know the landscape of where you live. There's something about knowing a place—not just the best places to eat or the best route to downtown, but really knowing the ins and outs of a location—that makes it home. And birders are good at that—better than most, actually. I can tell you within a few days when to start looking for Mississippi kites coursing over the oak tree–lined neighborhoods in the older part of my hometown. I can direct you to the best spot to listen for sora in the late-summer predawn, or the willow-lined pond by the airport where willow flycatchers show signs of nesting every year. These things are passed over by the nonbirders who live here, and they're worse off for living in ignorance.

We birders can know the real measure of a place. We know that there is nowhere on the planet that is truly unremarkable. Whether it is a Blackburnian warbler pausing at a city park on its way to Canada from South America or the seeming incongruity of a pair of barred owls nesting year after year in a patch of woods across from a shopping mall, there are little pieces of life everywhere, and birders are fortunate to be able to recognize them.

This fine-scale knowledge makes us better birders. It makes us better naturalists. I might even say it makes us better people if I were interested in being so cliché. We make trips down back roads and walk through forests in places we'd otherwise never visit, all in service of seeking out an extra bird in a far-flung county. All this creates a mosaic of individual bird sightings in the places we visit and where we live. It's a vast and intricate quilt of natural history, and every stitch is a tick on a county list.

TIPS
- eBird makes county listing easy and fun. Signing up is a breeze!
- Apps like Google Earth allow you to keep track of where you are at a very fine scale at any time.
- Instead of thinking about specific locations where you can find certain birds, think about habitats.
- Don't be afraid to get off the beaten path. There are untold birding hot spots still to be found!

NATE SWICK is the editor of the *ABA Blog* and author of *Birding for the Curious* and *The ABA Field Guide to Birds of the Carolinas*. His greatest birding ambition is to see at least a hundred species in each of North Carolina's one hundred counties. He lives in Greensboro, North Carolina, with his wife and two young children, all of whom are often unwitting accomplices in this quest.

Why I Love Birding in My Yard

by Michael O'Brien

My wife, Louise Zemaitis, and I built our house in 1999—a modest house on a rural street in West Cape May, New Jersey. Cape May, of course, is world-renowned for bird migration: a high-traffic site for tourists, but even more so for birds. Our yard sits among some excellent habitat: the Nature Conservancy's Cape May Migratory Bird Refuge ("the Meadows") is less than a mile to the south; Pond Creek Marsh is a similar distance to the northwest; and the Rea Farm ("the Beanery") is a short ways to the east. Right behind our house is a patch of wet woods, and in our backyard we manage a small meadow. From the vantage point of a second-story back porch (my favorite part of the house), we have a nice view of our meadow and of the sky to our north and east. I distinctly remember after closing the deal on the property, the first thing we did was head straight home to start working on the yard list. Northern cardinal was our first yard bird. There was never any question or discussion about whether we would keep a yard list. Of course we would!

I don't think of myself as a lister. Not that there's anything wrong with listing—that's just not usually my focus when I'm birding. But I do keep lists (these days, eBird keeps my lists for me), and my yard list is the one I find most rewarding. Louise and I are extremely fortunate to make a living traveling to some amazing places, guiding for Victor Emanuel Nature Tours. With all that travel, one might expect my favorite birding destination to be some far-flung place with lots of exotic, colorful birds. But as much as I love all the places I go, a highlight of every trip is coming home to see what's happening in the yard.

A big part of the appeal of yard birding is just getting a chance to catch my breath after being on the road. From the solitude of my back porch, with a warm cup of coffee in the morning, or a cold beer on a summer afternoon, I can enjoy many of the intellectual challenges of birding that I learn so much from—trying to identify distant birds, fly-bys, and a myriad of bird sounds—but with none of the pressures of "work birding." (As much as I love leading tours, keeping a diverse group of people happy can be stressful!)

From a learning perspective, I gain just as much by careful scrutiny of one location (patch birding) as I do from all my travels. I find it especially interesting to watch and listen to the ebb and flow of bird distribution and behavior, and savor those magical moments that mark the changing seasons.

Every month brings something special: American woodcocks *peent*ing on warm winter nights; the first laughing gulls flying over in March; Mississippi kites magically appearing overhead in May, drifting planktonically on northwest winds; the occasional least bittern or Virginia rail singing, just barely audible, from Pond Creek Marsh in June; terns commuting overland between feeding areas in the rips off Cape May Point to nesting grounds in the salt marsh behind Wildwood; those first overhead chip notes from yellow warbler and Louisiana waterthrush on a muggy mid-July dawn, marking the beginning of fall warbler migration; swarms of hummingbirds in our garden in late August; merlins hunting over our meadow during September dragonfly flights; skies full of hawks on those perfect October days; and floods of American robins passing through the yard on early November cold fronts.

I should point out that I'm a big fan of eBird, Cornell's online database of bird sightings, and I submit eBird sightings in my yard as often as possible. eBird makes it easy to keep methodical records, and the more you bird one location, the more interesting those amassed records become. One of the fun things about eBird is that you can create bar graphs for any birding location, with data displayed in one-week (quarter-month) increments. Although this may sound particularly geeky, whenever I'm home during a week that I'm usually away, I find myself "week listing" in the yard, trying to fill in gaps in coverage. Knowing that something *isn't* there is just as interesting as knowing that something *is* there. Are there really no red-tailed hawks in my yard during the second week of April, or have I just not spent enough time looking then?

The eBird bar graphs for my yard show some interesting patterns. For example, cedar waxwings occur through most of the year in my yard, but I have no records from late February to late April. This gap coincides with the leanest waxwing food supplies, both of their summer diet (insects) and their winter diet (berries). Baltimore oriole also shows an interesting temporal pattern. I see fall migrants regularly from mid-August to mid-September, but also a separate small peak in November and early December. These late-fall birds seem to be "reverse migrants," drifting back north on strong southwesterly winds. (As a side note, these late-season Baltimore orioles are good indicators that other species—much rarer ones, such as ash-throated flycatcher—may have drifted up from the southwest on the same winds.) Even something as mundane as Canada goose, a common year-round species in Cape May, can show interesting patterns. Although flocks or pairs fly over my house nearly every day, the only geese I record in my yard from early June to mid-July are birds heard calling in the distance. When geese molt their flight feathers, they go flightless for a month or so, which is why they don't fly over my house then.

Of course, when it comes to yard birding, it's hard to beat the excitement of adding a rarity to the list. Over the years, we've seen quite a few, but several rise to the top as most memorable: a little gull flying low overhead in March, just days after we settled on the property; a black rail audible from our bedroom window as it sang in the Cape May Meadows one June evening; a band-tailed pigeon that appeared at our neighbor's feeder one January day; a late-September zone-tailed hawk that sailed overhead before flying across the bay to Delaware; and an incredible November flock of Franklin's gulls that I raced home just in time to see from my porch as they flew west over the Meadows. And in the category of stupid things I'll never do again, there was the time I got sooty shearwater on the yard list, but nearly killed myself climbing on the rooftop, the only way to see a tiny sliver of ocean from our property

Okay, maybe I am a lister, at least sometimes.

TIPS: What You Need to Enjoy Yard Birding
- Binoculars (to see birds better)
- Merlin app or field guide (to identify unknown birds)
- Larkwire app (create a playlist to learn backyard bird sounds)
- eBird app (to submit sightings and organize your records)

>>•<<

MICHAEL O'BRIEN is an author, artist, VENT tour leader, and associate naturalist for Cape May Bird Observatory, and has a passionate interest in migration, bird sounds, and field identification. He is coauthor of *The Shorebird Guide* and *Flight Calls of Migratory Birds,* and primary author of the birdsong learning app Larkwire. His illustrations can be seen in the National Geographic and Peterson Field Guides.

Why I Love Spectrograms

by Nathan Pieplow

MY GRANDPARENTS OWNED A CABIN IN THE BLACK HILLS of South Dakota. In that cabin was an old dictionary, and in that old dictionary was a page of alphabets.

It was a full-page chart of the Greek, Russian, Arabic, Hebrew, and Hindi scripts, with each symbol displayed beside its approximate English pronunciation. It captivated me, not just because of the striking, exotic shapes of the foreign letters, but because each of those shapes was soaked through with mysterious *meaning*. Each alphabet was a secret code that millions of people in another part of the world were actually using, every day.

These days, I find myself fascinated by another collection of striking shapes and mysterious meanings. This time, it's the alphabet of the birds—the computer-generated graphs of bird sounds called *spectrograms*.

Birders might not be accustomed to thinking of spectrograms as alphabetic. But *a spectrogram is text,* not in metaphor but in fact. Just like this sentence, a spectrogram is the written representation of an oral communication. Just as the lines and curves that make up this sentence are standing in for sounds, so do the lines and the curves in a spectrogram—and in both cases, each line and curve carries meaning to those who speak the language in which the text was composed.

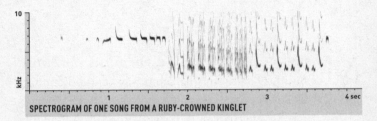

SPECTROGRAM OF ONE SONG FROM A RUBY-CROWNED KINGLET

I love spectrograms for their meaning. They encode a bird's intentions; they draw its inner state. Each species has its own symbols for aggression, alarm, sexual ardor, and the hunger of begging nestlings. To those who know the code, spectrograms explain what a bird is doing and why.

I love spectrograms for their mystery. There is much we do not know about bird sounds, even those of some common and widespread species. How many songs does an individual brown thrasher sing? How many whistled calls do Lapland longspurs have? Spectrograms, someday, could tell us.

Above all, I love spectrograms for their beauty. Some spectrograms match human calligraphy, flourish for flourish, in intricacy, tension, balance, and grace. Just as each calligrapher's work displays its own style, each vocalizing bird traces an individually unique spectrogram when it sings—its own personal signature in sound, the result of a fleeting, even if repeated, intersection of communicator, medium, and meaning. The best explanation I've found comes from the *Wikipedia* entry on *shodo* (Japanese calligraphy): "For any particular piece of paper, the calligrapher has but one chance to create with the brush . . . The brush writes a statement about the calligrapher at a moment in time." In the same way, the spectrogram writes a statement about a bird at the moment it utters a sound.

And there's one other reason I love spectrograms. For me, spectrograms are security. One day, sooner than I would like, I may depend on them for the very continuation of my birding career.

Age-related hearing loss runs in my family, and I've been noticing its onset for several years now. Last spring, I heard a strange, unfamiliar chatter from high in a fir tree. I excitedly slipped on my headphones and aimed my microphone at the treetop. When the sound rang out again, greatly amplified, I was shocked to hear the familiar song of a golden-crowned kinglet. My traitorous ears had been filtering out all the high notes, leaving only ragged pieces of the sound. It's this way with a lot of birds now. The *tsip* notes of chickadees escape me. Blue-gray gnatcatchers remain somehow silent until they are no more than twenty feet away.

But if I plug my microphone into my computer, or into

a smartphone, I can open up a program that generates a real-time scrolling spectrogram of all the audio picked up by the mic. The machine listens to the world for me and translates it into a text I can read.

If I do someday lose the ability to hear the birds, I know that I'll be able to watch their signatures scroll past on the screen: the elegant autographs of meadowlarks, the graffiti tags of grackles, the intricate calligraphy of a skylarking bobolink. All of them will sign their names, over and over, in the unmistakable handwriting of their species. And I'll read them with the same joy that I get from recognizing a bird by its plumage pattern or its shape. I'll be able to stay connected with the birds through a form of social media, all my old friends writing me messages in real time.

I love spectrograms because they mean I don't need good ears to enjoy bird sounds. Sounds are ineffable and fleeting; spectrograms are legible and collectible. Like the alphabets in my grandparents' dictionary, they are a secret code that I never tire of learning to crack.

TIPS for Learning to Read Spectrograms
- Search http://ebird.org/media for any bird species, and click to play any audio recording. A spectrogram of the sound will scroll past as the audio plays. If you upload your own recording to an eBird checklist, eBird will automatically generate its spectrogram for you.

- Search your app store for "spectrogram" to see the variety of available apps to create spectrograms out of real-time audio or sound files.
- For further reading on this topic, see *The Singing Life of Birds* by Donald Kroodsma; *The Sound Approach to Birding* by Mark Constantine and The Sound Approach; and the *Peterson Field Guide to Bird Sounds* by the author of this essay.

NATHAN PIEPLOW is the author of the *Peterson Field Guide to Bird Sounds*. An avid bird sound recordist, he runs the bird sound blog Earbirding.com. He is a cocreator of the Colorado Birding Trail and former editor of the journal *Colorado Birds*. He teaches writing and rhetoric at the University of Colorado in Boulder.

Birding the World
EVERYTHING OLD IS NEW AGAIN

by Noah Strycker

AFTER GRADUATING FROM HIGH SCHOOL, I TOOK MY FIRST birding trip abroad. I'd been obsessed by birds since the fifth grade, and it was getting tough to find new species around home. So I signed on to a research project studying bird nests in Panama, and took off for the jungles of Central America.

The memory of my first day in Panama comes back to me now as crisp and clear as if it were yesterday. When I woke up, I looked out the window and saw eight life birds at once. Later that morning, while walking through the rainforest, I realized I could not recognize a single bird sound in the tropical chorus. It was overwhelming and exciting: at home, I had become so used to identifying every chip note that I'd forgotten what it feels like to be a beginner. To my eager eyes, even the common Panamanian birds seemed vivid and extraordinary. Ruddy ground-doves were painted in saturated sienna. Blue-gray tanagers sparkled cobalt in the sky. And the dainty common tody-flycatchers built nests like long, matted beards hanging from trees that bore fruits I'd never heard of.

Since then, I've visited almost fifty countries on seven continents, and I have found that feeling like a beginner never gets old, when all is filled with wonderful possibilities. Birding far from home is a form of time travel, a trip into a past when you knew less but noticed more. Remember the surprises you experienced when you first started watching birds, how beautiful they first seemed? Those days might seem far gone, but they are as close as a ticket to someplace new.

The beauty of birds is that they are everywhere, from the deepest wildernesses to the most crowded inner cities. Even apparently lifeless places lie within their reach: birds have been recorded at the South Pole, above the summit of Mount Everest, and hundreds of miles from the nearest land. Because they can fly, they have a more three-dimensional view than we do, and some birds live almost entirely in the air. The common swift, for instance, which migrates from Europe to Africa, is thought to alight only at its nest; it spends the entire rest of its life on the wing. Albatrosses routinely glide all the way around the southern ocean, with the wind at their tails, and were doing so eons before we humans first realized that the Earth is round.

For me, birding offers a fresh way to see the world. When I travel, I try to think like a bird, and this helps me soak in more than a regular sightseer might. A bird defines its surroundings in terms of natural features: forests, mountains, oceans, deserts, valleys, ice caps, rivers, prairies, lakes, and so on. When I transport my mind aloft, I am no longer a visitor; I am an eagle, looking down on the landscape with crystal vision. Beneath my wings, human civilization begins to seem relatively insignificant.

Just imagine what the world must look like from a bird's-eye view. How do our feathered friends regard this planet as they go about their daily lives? Birds inhabit many of the same places we do, but they probably interpret their surroundings a bit differently. We might learn a thing or two from their perspective.

For starters, birds wouldn't have much patience with our world's political divisions. National borders convey little meaning in the avian way of life, and a bird would have to puzzle over the many different lines and colors on a map. What would a Swainson's hawk make of all the documents required to complete its annual migration across international boundaries from Canada to Argentina? Good thing birds don't need passports or visas.

I like to think about this stuff when I take trips to other countries. Birds are global citizens, free to come and go as they please, and in this way they exist on a different plane from our own. To really appreciate the meaning of "free as a bird," it helps to do a little traveling yourself. No matter where you go, birding gives you focus and context, turning any tourist trip into a treasure quest. There is nothing like venturing beyond familiar borders to give you a new, bird's-eye view of the world.

Watching birds in foreign places comes with one other great benefit: it encourages the appreciation of birds on their own terms and on their own turf. Close to home, birders often seek out birds merely because they appear on one side of some humanly defined border—within a particular county or state or area. Some birders go to extreme lengths to add new species to their border-driven lists, and I've done my share of chasing rarities. But this kind of birding depends on a geographic system that has nothing intrinsically to do with birds, making it difficult to tease out the interesting observations from the thirst for novelty. When you visit a new place, the slate is wiped clean, and the birds appear afresh as colorful, compelling creatures instead of checkmarks on a list.

As much as anything, birding without borders is a state of mind. To recapture the wonder of birds, you don't have to travel to a far-flung destination—but you do have to put some effort into it. Try this at home: the next time you see a common bird species flying overhead, picture to yourself what the world looks like from its point of view, as if it were giving you a tour of your own neighborhood. Or, even better, take some new birders under your wing and guide them around your local patch. Showing someone a lifer is as good as finding one yourself. It is as if, by looking at birds through another set of eyes, you see your own world again for the first time.

TIPS for Birding the World

- Study up ahead of time. Get a field guide for the area you'll be visiting, look up which birds are common there (the free online eBird resource is excellent for this purpose), and learn their field marks before you arrive. A treasure hunt is more fun when you know what you're looking for.
- Connect with locals. These days, birders are everywhere, and reaching out to the local birders is a good way to make new friends while traveling. Expect to at least cover expenses for anyone who takes you into the field. BirdingPal.org is a good place to start.
- Remember that it's not just about the birds. Foreign travel encompasses all kinds of experiences, so don't be afraid to spend time soaking up cultures, landscapes, and other sights along the way. Like a bird, you are an ambassador on the wing!

Noah Strycker is associate editor of *Birding* magazine, the author of the books *Among Penguins* and *The Thing with Feathers*, a regular contributor to bird magazines, a popular speaker and blogger, and a naturalist guide for expedition cruises to Antarctica and the Arctic. Based in Oregon, he has studied birds on all seven continents, and in 2015 set a big year world record. Visit his website at www.noahstrycker.com.

The Where-tos and When-tos
of Birding

by Pete Dunne

Wで HAT I LIKE MOST ABOUT BIRDING IS ENGAGING BIRDS
in their natural environment. Knowing where and
when to go increases my opportunities to engage a diversity
of species. And that is one of the biggest differences between
an experienced birder and a new birder: not identification
acumen, but temporal and situational awareness.

More specifically, experienced birders know where and
when to go to take advantage of the seasonal reapportion-
ment of birds and recognize weather conditions that make a
particular location or species-focus productive. So informed,
they can plan their weekend outings accordingly. Beginning
birders tend to simply go to the same local hot spot over and
over, grateful for the birds they find but generally unmind-
ful of the cause-and-effect relationship that causes birds to be
where they are, when they are.

With experience, birders learn that midsummer is a relatively unproductive time to search for breeding woodland

songbirds. Most species are still on territory so are not concentrated or moving freely. They are also typically quiet, not vocalizing, so difficult to find. In midsummer, many experienced birders turn their attention instead to southbound shorebirds that will be attracted to local sod farms, sewage treatment facilities, and reservoirs offering mud-rimmed shorelines. Experienced birders also know that midsummer cold fronts propel migrating shorebirds south.

A number of other conditions may prompt birds to suddenly appear.

- Drought conditions in a species' normal breeding range. For example, drought conditions in the Southeast may prompt wading birds like wood stork and white ibis to catch the Gumbo Express and ride the warm winds of summer north in search of open water and aquatic fare.
- Storms, which are nature's way of reshuffling the deck. A wall of rain during migration will cause migrants to drop into the nearest available proper habitat.
- Rain. Migrating songbirds caught in rain inundate woodlands; waterfowl and other aquatic species suddenly appear on inland lakes.
- Hurricanes, which are the East Coast birder's friend, ferrying rare tropical (usually pelagic) species in the eye of the storm, depositing them on inland lakes where the eye crosses land.

So how do inexperienced birders learn the where-tos and when-tos of birding? The obvious answer is through experience.

But beginning birders can shortcut the learning process by relying upon the institutional memory of the local birding network. Join the local bird club, and listen to the counsel of the tribal elders who have done it all before and to the hot young turks who are doing it now with energy and fervor. Go on the club's organized field trips—you can bet that they are timed and calibrated to take advantage of the best birding opportunities the region and calendar have to offer. Your local nature center's field trip calendar will also be seasonally calibrated.

So, too, will the birding column in your local paper, as well as the weekly offerings of your favorite local blogger. Writers are always strapped for subject matter. Most fall back on the tried-and-true formula of following the calendar. If it's April, the writer's subject will be "Waves of Neotropical migrants—where and when to find 'em." If it's September, and you live in New England, the subject will be migrating broad-winged hawks and tips for placing yourself in position to catch the 10,000-bird flight. If it's July, and you live in southeast Arizona, the subject will be which Mexican hummingbirds are turning up at what feeders. If it's November, and you live in California, the subject will be finding eastern warbler vagrants at a desert migrant trap near you.

Of course, if you enjoy simply birding your local patch weekend after weekend, that's perfectly fine. I do it myself. Bird watching is more than a point-to-point search for rare birds. You can learn a great deal about the cause-and-effect relationship between birds, weather, and seasonality by simply studying your hometown favorites. You'll learn when they arrive, when they depart, what they forage upon at different times of the season, and what other bird species they team up with—all of which is really cool stuff, worth your study. It may not get you the bird club's award for biggest year list, but it ain't a half-bad way to enjoy birds.

And who knows, maybe the eye of the hurricane will pass right over your local patch. Wouldn't you love to turn up at the club banquet with images of your bananaquit? But you are advised to post notice and photos of the bird before it disappears. Many birders look askance at finding out about local rarities after the fact, and as a new birder, you'll want to stay in the good graces of the club.

TIPS for Finding Birds
- First, you need to be where the birds are. Get out there. Good plans that are never realized are called lost opportunities.
- Second, use binoculars that are designed to facilitate bird finding—binoculars that offer a generous field of view, good depth of field, and a nimble focus, and are,

of course, optically precise. Nobody has ever purchased a quality birding binocular and regretted it.

- Third, resist the temptation to slam the binoculars to your eyes at the first hint of a bird. Take in the big picture first. See the bird in context, then augment this awareness with a magnified slice of the world.

P ETE DUNNE forged a bond with nature as a child and has been studying hawks for more than forty years. He has written fifteen books and countless magazine and newspaper columns. He was the founding director of the Cape May Bird Observatory and now serves as New Jersey Audubon's birding ambassador.

Conservation Cooperation

by Dorian Anderson

P EOPLE COLLECT ALL SORTS OF THINGS—BASEBALL CARDS, stamps, dolls, and coins being popular. I collect birds, or, more specifically, sightings of and stories about birds, as I bird-watch my way through my particular corner of the world. Bird watching is how I interact with the natural world, my window to an incredibly diverse and beautiful group of animals. From albatrosses and penguins to hummingbirds and warblers, the number of evolutionary permutations on the avian theme is astounding. It is precisely this diversity that motivates me; I want to see them all.

I am, however, very concerned about the future of birds and other animals. Each day more land is apportioned for human use and development. This leaves less functional habitat intact for natural purposes. As the human tide with its associated environmental and ecological degradation is unlikely to crest anytime soon, the pressure on birds and their habitats is only going to increase. Birders and other outdoor enthusiasts must take an active role in habitat conservation if birds are to thrive.

Thinking about these environmental concerns, in 2013 I resigned my position as a postdoctoral fellow in neurobiology at Harvard Medical School and Massachusetts General Hospital to ride my bike around the country in search of birds. The idea of an environmentally sustainable, nationwide bird search was so unique, so crazy that I thought my life would be incomplete should routine, expectation, or fear dissuade me from undertaking it. On January 1, 2014, I boarded my bicycle for what eventually became an 18,000-mile ride. In the next year, I visited twenty-eight states, observed 618 bird species, raised nearly $50,000 for habitat conservation, and highlighted in my daily blog issues of conservation and environmental sustainability. The adventure pushed me beyond my known physical and mental limits and introduced me to hundreds of new people—birders and others—around the country. It was the sort of adventure that is usually relegated to the imagination.

One of the people I met on my journey was Gene, the owner and administrator of a duck hunting lodge in the backwaters of Anahuac, Texas. I had been put in touch with Gene through some locals who thought he might be able to house me at the lodge for a few days. I was, admittedly, very apprehensive about the prospect of staying at a hunting lodge; I do not condone or understand the killing of animals in the name of sport. The only hunting I can accept is that for food or population control, which, in this age of pizza delivery and vanishing species, generally rules out anything other than deer. Despite the potential conflict of interest, Gene graciously offered me a bed for three nights. He also said that I could have free run at whatever I could find in the fully stocked kitchen for the duration of my stay. Perpetually hungry and generally out of other options on my bike, "all-I-could-eat" was all I needed to hear.

Gene met me out front when I arrived. He was in his fifties, in good shape, a still-thick, golden white mass of hair perched above his round, pale face. Eyes narrow, jowls less so, he greeted me with a smile and firm handshake. He had an appropriately Texan drawl, and his jovial, backslapping personality suggested we'd get along perfectly—provided we could avoid a debate about the morality of hunting.

Dispensing with introductions and pleasantries, Gene escorted me into the lodge where hung the mounted bodies of dozens of stuffed waterfowl and the heads of several ungulates—moose, elk, and deer among them. A stuffed beaver peered lifelessly from the mantle, and a motionless javelina stood silent vigil in the room's corner. It was a museum of death, a monument to man's power over beast. Mostly, though, it was sad, sad to see such incredible creatures reduced to decorations on a par with curtains or accent pillows. The bunkroom in which Gene placed me was, thankfully, free of such adornment, and I unpacked my stuff before passing out for the next few hours.

I awoke to the smell of sausage. Shaking off my rather extended nap, I found Gene grilling away on the back porch, corn on the cob and green beans going strong on the stove. He invited me to sit and join him. He asked about my adventure to date. He, like most, thought I was certifiably insane, but he did recognize my love of the outdoors and passion for birds.

"Must be pretty weird for you to be in a hunting lodge, huh?"

"Yeah, I'm more used to seeing these guys flying around."

"I've recently started learning the local birds besides the ducks. There's a lotta stuff out there."

"I'll confess, I just don't get the whole hunting thing. I'd much rather hang a photo of a still-living duck on my wall than a stuffed, once-living one."

"I can understand that. I am actually starting to get into bird photography as well. It's really tough. Gun's easier."

We both laughed. We spent the remainder of the evening conversing about a wide range of topics—photography, hunting, birding, and habitat conservation among them. What I came to appreciate was that Gene's feelings and attitudes about the natural world closely mirrored my own. His time in the hunting blind, usually very early in the morning before most were awake, was as spiritual and therapeutic for him as was early-morning bird watching for me. He explained that as a duck hunter, he was very committed to preserving the wetlands in which that activity took place. Without wetlands, there wouldn't be anywhere to hunt ducks.

Riding through miles of pristine wetlands at the Anahuac National Wildlife Refuge the following day, I thought back to our conversation. Although many birders are never going to fully understand the motivations for duck hunting, we would be advised to engage hunters on the conservation front. As habitat loss affects both birders and hunters, we will be best leveraged to stem the rising developmental tide together. Protected habitat will, at the end of it all, benefit both hunted and nonhunted species, and it is in that protected habitat where future generations of birders will be awed by the beauty and diversity of birds. Presented with a choice between a wildlife refuge that permits hunting or a strip of beachfront condominiums, I know which one I would choose.

TIPS

- Birding can be as big an adventure as a person wants it to be.
- Birders (and everyone, really) benefit when we behave in environmentally conscious ways.
- When birders connect with other groups of people (such as hunters), our combined impact on conservation is greater.

>▷ • ◁<

DORIAN ANDERSON starting birding in Philadelphia at age seven. In 2014, he completed the first nationwide bicycle big year, finding 618 species along his 18,000-mile route. He holds a B.S. from Stanford in molecular biology and a Ph.D. from NYU in developmental genetics and molecular and cellular biology. He currently resides in Los Angeles and works as a researcher at the University of Southern California. He is writing a book about his bike trip.

Soul Food
Wild Turkeys and Wandering Warblers

by J. Drew Lanham

I'VE BEEN BIRDING SINCE THE SECOND GRADE AND HUNTING white-tailed deer and wild turkeys since I was twenty-two. Both are important ways for me to experience nature and understand my place in it. Watching spring migrants filter back into greening woods from miraculous migratory journeys while I wait for a wild turkey to make enough of a mistake to commit to my dinner table isn't really a contradiction for me. An ovenbird singing overhead reminds me that another spring season is underway. It's all about renewal, and in that little bird's song is hope for future springs. Hunting is a way for me to use my woodsman's skills and occasionally feed my family. For me, both are food for my nature-loving soul.

After twenty years of chasing and only two turkeys taken, I strike out and come home empty-handed 90 percent of the time, shotgun unfired, turkey tags still neatly tucked away, and longbeards none the worse for wear. Trying to beat the sun to the birds hasn't been successful, and so recently, with another "O'fer" turkey season in the balance, it was time to change things up. The idea of the midmorning start is to let nature take its course. Let the birds do their thing off the roost and in the pastures. Then, after all the loving is done, intercept the still-stimulated gobblers as they cruise the woods for the hens that would be taking a break from nest tending.

Heartened as always by new chances to learn and improve my wood skills, I assured myself that today would be the day. I imagined the hunt in a river bottom where I would call the bird in on a magnetic string of the raspiest, most alluring turkey hen love notes that no self-respecting gobbler could resist. From somewhere on the oak ridge above the river, the lovelorn gobbler would answer with his thunderous pleas for a meeting. He would stroll in, all puffed up with his head glowing red, white, and blue. Spitting, drumming, and fanning his tail in and out of the shadows of buttressed trees, his gobbling would shake the ground and my heart would thump in time with the rhythm of the woods. In a cathedral of hardwoods, the wild world would stop to listen.

And then, only after I'd watched every bit of the show and the boss deflated to survey the scene, I'd pull the trigger. Afterward, kneeling in respect beside him, I'd stroke the obsidian iridescence of the magnificent plumage, feel the sharpness of the spurs, and inspect the evidence of work done to win the chance at making the next generation of *Meleagris gallopavo:* tattered wingtips rubbed to frazzles and fan ragged from combatting with other toms and cavorting with hens. And then, with the day done, I'd sling the old longbeard over my shoulder as I walked out of the spring woods. His sacrifice would mean a soon-to-come satisfying meal, gathered, like the autumn venison I enjoy, to continue the circle of sustenance among family and friends.

That was the scene I imagined, anyway. It's a dream I've relived in and out of the April wild turkey season. That day, like almost every time before, it was not to be. As I wandered in the woods, the trident tracks and leaves thrown about were the evidence of things not seen. In vain attempts to bedazzle the birds, I called insistently but got only a token, distant gobble or two that sounded more like an uncertain young Jake than the superconfident Boss Tom I was after. I wandered and fell into the rhythm of the woods, with the distraction of other birds easing the pain of another failure.

I made my way down to the river. Big trees—splotch-skinned sycamores, gigantic sweetgum, and the occasional towering loblolly—crowded the bottomland forest like sylvan columns. The forest floor was littered with tangles of Virginia creeper and painted buckeye. It was open enough to let a turkey feel secure but with enough cover to hide me from the wariest eyes in the woods. I found a pretty sit at the foot of a big shagbark hickory. I settled in and let the shadows collect around me. I felt invisible and hoped the turkeys would buy in. I called softly—*yelp yelp yelp yelp*—hoping it sounded sexy, but the turkeys didn't seem to think so.

The dawn chorus was peaking. A pair of Kentucky warblers dueled along the creek, throwing their rollicking songs back and forth—*per-deep, per-deep, per-deep, per-deep per-deep!*—to proclaim a stretch of the scrubby cane and privet that might foster the next brood of yellow-bellied, black-masked skulkers. The Kentuckys were joined by a who's who of Neotropical migrant birddom. A Louisiana waterthrush whistled along the waterway. A wood thrush fluted song from higher up on the ridge as a summer tanager *picky-ticky-tuck*ed its way into the fray. A rose-breasted grosbeak clip-called somewhere nearby as a yellow-billed cuckoo—what the old-timers called a rain crow—croaked a forecast that seemed bound for failure on such a sunny day.

Spring after spring, the birds that wing their way from their tropical equatorial winter homes to find refuge and the chance to make more of themselves during the breeding season, in stands of timber or throngs of tangles that nurtured them the year before, inspire me. The drive to migrate across hemispheres by a two-ounce warbler or to strut, spit, and drum like a twenty-pound gobbler is all for the same purpose: to make more. Caught up in the "other" bird din, I almost forgot why I'd come. I called again for the one bird I'd not heard from, and this time, a gobble! Someone *was* paying attention!

I dropped to the ground and tried my best to make like a tree stump. I called again, adrenaline pumping, but just as suddenly, there was nothing. The minutes slogged by and a wandering neon green inchworm—warbler food—measured itself against the idle expanse of my trigger finger. As my backside numbed and the adrenalin drained, the dream did too. A northern parula zipped its song up the scale and the cuckoo croaked as if the rain were a sure thing. I had a lengthy bird list for the morning. It just didn't include a wild turkey dinner.

Another failure? No, when I really think about it, it was another success! Perhaps there's too much going on in the spring woods that makes me a less-than-competent turkey hunter. With all the new arrivals, I can't resist sneaking a peak at the flashes of fresh feathers or turning to see the bird belting out some territorial solo so close by. A simple head turn or even eyes widened to gawk at the undeniable beauty of something as stunning as a prothonotary would be a stop sign for a turkey, which would see such things from a hundred yards away.

On most hunting days, I let my birder get the best of me. I always take a bird list from the woods; seldom do I take a life. Although the stats didn't improve that day for me (I'm sure the turkeys didn't mind), I left fulfilled. Birding and hunting are soul food for me. They're both nature-seeking quests that always give more than I can ever take away.

In the afterglow of sighting a redstart returning from a winter in the tropics or being sustained by the game meat I occasionally take, there's a reconnection with nature by sight, sound, and sustenance.

What does hunting have to do with birding? A great deal. For many like me, hunting builds the bonds to conserving in ways that benefit many more lives than are ever taken. Warblers, whitetails, and multitudes of other wild things are the beneficiaries of the millions of bottom-line dollars that come from hunting licenses and taxes on firearms, ammunition, and archery tackle. Perhaps the closest connection that birders have to hunters is through the funds that come from sales of federal duck stamps, which are at the core of building and maintaining our national wildlife refuge system. I'm not a duck hunter, but each year, along with thousands of other birders, I purchase the Migratory Bird Hunting and Conservation Stamp to support the acquisition and maintenance of millions of acres of public refuge lands that support not only huntable waterfowl but also legions of other bird species that will only ever have binoculars and spotting scopes aimed at them. In the end, it's about enjoying wild places and wild things. Both need commitments to conserve. If conservation is to be successful in the future, both groups of outdoor enthusiasts will need to unite in the common cause.

Together, there's much work for birders and hunters to do together as ethical stewards of the land. I'm lucky to live the life of one who finds soul sustenance in both ventures. As I return home from hunting almost every time with nothing more than memories, I know that connecting as many lovers of wildness together as possible in concerted effort can only make conservation stronger. And that's the best thing for the birds—warblers and wild turkeys alike!

TIPS

- Read up and find out about the shared roots between hunting and birding. Famous birder/hunter/conservationists include John James Audubon, Presidents Theodore Roosevelt and Jimmy Carter, father of wildlife conservation Aldo Leopold, and birding royalty Pete Dunne. Some great resources for understanding connections are Leopold's *A Sand County Almanac,* Peter Matthiessen's classic *Wildlife in North America,* and Scott Weidensaul's *Of a Feather.*

- Buy a federal duck stamp and, if available, a state nongame stamp that supports wildlife and habitat conservation. Funds are dedicated to public lands and many more species than those that are hunted.

- Get permission from a deer-hunting friend to watch the wild world from the elevated perspective of a tree stand outside of the hunting season. Use every safety precaution, such as a safety harness—take your bins and camera and enjoy the high!

- Ask a waterfowler questions about duck identification. Most have amazing long-distance identification abilities, and in some states they must pass proficiency tests before they can hunt. Their skills at gestalt ID will make you a better birder.

J. DREW LANHAM is an Alumni Distinguished Professor and Master Teacher at Clemson University. In his work of "coloring the conservation conversation" and "connecting the conservation dots," he uses birds as vehicles to promote human-nature synergy. A lifelong birder and adult-onset hunter, he's watched birds in forty-three states and abroad in South Africa and South America. He lives in Seneca, South Carolina, and claims the birds with feathers as favorites.

In Defense of Gull Watching

by Amar Ayyash

INHABITING ALL OF THE EARTH'S CONTINENTS, GULLS ARE a diverse group of only fifty-two species, yet they've likely spawned more identification debates than the rest of the world's bird taxa combined. Some larids, mainly subadults, can't be bothered with conforming to the plates and photos used in our field guides. A remarkable amount of variation at the species level elicits a wide range of feelings among birders, from anger and despair to thrilling gratification. A love-hate relationship is my best way of describing the situation.

There's a certain subculture that exists in birding that generally sways birders from delving into this group altogether. Beginning birders are often given the impression that they're to stay away from the dark abyss of gulls—namely, four-year gulls (so-called large white-headed gulls). Those species are said to be the work of the devil. Countless times I've heard birders remark that "gulls are impossible" and "too hard" to identify. After hearing this enough times, a birder can be overcome with a defeatist attitude, and sadly some—including birders with decades of experience—never get around to sufficiently learning how to identify the gulls they see.

Large gulls often get a bad rap because of their propensity for hybridizing (catalysts of evolution, if you will). Remarkably, various hybrid combinations can at times do a good job of mimicking other species (and at times a flock might look like a thousand-piece jigsaw puzzle of a grassy field). As I was writing this essay, I was interrupted by an urgent message with the subject "North America's First-Record Mediterranean Gull." It took only a few seconds of looking over the photos to see that, instead, the photographer had found a ring-billed × black-headed gull hybrid. Adrenaline rush over.

These crossbreeds drive some birders nuts for one of two reasons: (1) hybrids are perceived as a "waste" because they don't "count" on checklists, and (2) hybrids create a level of discomfort for observers because they can't be pigeonholed in a neat "species box." To the former I say, feel free to make addenda to your lists. It's okay. To the latter, know that nature and living organisms in particular are far more than a set of disjoint boxes. Nature evolves, and hybridization (or lack thereof) is a key ingredient. But the truth is, most gulls are comfortably identifiable as to species.

Experienced gull watchers and pro-ninja birders are moved by anomalous individuals that don't fit the norm. Enthusiastic disputations on size, structure, and feather pattern minutiae can quickly confuse someone new to gulls, but this shouldn't discourage you. Your commitment to learning how to identify gulls doesn't have to be centered around these nuances (unless this piques your interest). Identifying gulls is analytic in nature, and to this end there's something here for birders of every skill level. Skills learned through gull ID can be applied to other families of birds, and this contributes to becoming a better birder.

When I first began to develop an interest in watching gulls, I asked a trusted expert in the field what advice he had for taking on this challenging family of birds. His response was simple: "Commit yourself to the common species first—learn them well and be keen on aging them." This guidance was insightful and proved to be momentous. It's easy to look past species that we see in abundance (for me, those species are ring-billed gull and herring gull), but they are, in fact, the best way to become comfortable with gull identification. Get intimately familiar with your common species if you want a solid footing!

Finding gulls is relatively easy. Their ability to capitalize on nearly all habitats and food sources—including their willingness to avail themselves of our waste at landfills—makes them hard to miss. I recommend starting with exercises as simple as sitting in your car and studying your local flock in a mall parking lot or beachfront. Inland reservoirs and dams are other great sites to consider. It will take a certain level of discipline to force yourself to spend time watching common species. The idea behind this is to know your local gulls so well that you'll immediately be able to spot something out of the ordinary. Rare gulls are almost always found in flocks of common gulls, and your charge is to pick out the diamond in the rough.

For many, a big part of the fascination with gulls is the ability to "age" them with some degree of accuracy. Sooner or later, you'll encounter an ID that hinges on being able to first properly age the bird in question. Begin by focusing on adult birds, as this age group is mostly cohesive and shows the least amount of variation when compared to the other age groups. Then take on *first-cycle* birds. Having a basic knowledge of feather topography and molt cycles will make the experience of watching gulls (and birds in general) much more rewarding. Although it's not a prerequisite, this basic knowledge aids in our ability to communicate and allows us to read identification literature with more ease. Attending a gull field trip where you can see these species and their different age groups pointed out to you in the field will be of great benefit and lots of fun.

TIPS

For the most part, gulls are accommodating, loafing in the open for long periods of time. They're much easier to study than small birds skulking in the bush. With adequate exposure and time invested, it is possible to learn how to identify most of the gulls that we encounter. Let's summarize with a few key points:

- Get as close as you can—with some patience, you'll find gulls often allow close approach.
- Focus on your most common species first, preferably adults.
- Learn feather topography and molt.
- Join others in watching gulls.
- Think of gull ID as an opportunity to become a better birder.

A MAR AYYASH devotes much of his time to watching and photographing gulls. Both an expert on gull identification and an evangelist for "gull recreation," he hosts several websites devoted to gulling and has published various technical articles on the subject. Amar serves on the board of directors of the Illinois Ornithological Society and also coordinates the annual Gull Frolic.

THE PLOT OF THIS MOVIE IS TOTALLY RIDICULOUS

Birding
WINDEX FOR THE SOUL

by Greg Miller

T HE PEOPLE WHO KNOW ME USUALLY ASSOCIATE MY name with one of the characters in the 2011 movie *The Big Year*. I was the real-life birder portrayed by Jack Black. And a few of you have read the nonfiction book the movie was based on, *The Big Year* by Mark Obmascik (2004). The movie says I did my big year because I wanted to make something out of my life. But really, I did the big year for a less ambitious reason—my life was a wreck.

I often jokingly tell audiences that the most selfish and irresponsible year of my life is now the most celebrated. And that is simultaneously funny and sad. All the important things in my life were shaken in the 1990s. I resigned as an assistant pastor of my church to save my marriage. I was still working full-time as a computer programmer, which didn't leave much time to be home. Not only was I unable to salvage my marriage, but I had to leave a job that I had planned to do for the rest of my life—and I had to physically move, too.

The emotional pressures were traumatic for me. I felt crushed. My esteem lay before me in a thousand pieces. The damage seemed irreparable. My dreams all faded, and hope was gone. What reason was there to live? At my lowest point, I contemplated suicide.

Only a handful of positive truths still remained inside me. I remembered an old inspirational message from the late Robert Schuller. In essence, he said, "Don't look at what you have *lost*. Look at what you have *left*." It was a great message about how to deal with devastating loss. So I encouraged myself by looking inside to find what was there. And all I could see was birding.

It was my dad who got me into birding at a very early age. How early? Young enough that I cannot remember my very first pair of binoculars. My fondest years were those going birding with my dad. We shared a passion.

As a former schoolteacher, I also understood the power of distraction to change a child's thinking, at least temporarily. And I knew myself. I could avoid wallowing around in the quagmire of self-pity if I could replace negative thoughts with anything positive.

So it dawned on me: I could use birding to distract myself.

Sometimes I find myself veering toward spontaneity, and occasionally I set myself on an extreme course. Rather than just a little bit of birding, I decided to go for all the marbles—what's known as a *big year*. It's an attempt to see as many species of birds as possible in one calendar year in the forty-eight contiguous states, all of Canada, and Alaska (the American Birding Association's "ABA Area").

I threw myself into the endeavor while maintaining a full-time job as a computer programmer for a nuclear power plant. My plan to avoid self-pity by replacing it with a fun distraction worked quite well. I saw 715 species of birds, traveled over 135,000 miles, and met hundreds of friendly birders who helped me achieve an epic year.

What really happened? Why did this work? There were a number of things that added to my ultimate success, most of which happened despite my simple plans.

- I love birds. Their world is like a parallel universe to ours. When I go birding I enter into their world and leave mine behind. I see a cardinal singing. It doesn't care about the latest presidential race. It hasn't heard about wars. Or murders. Or Hollywood. It doesn't know my life. It doesn't know where I came from. It doesn't know my family. But it is singing. It's beautiful. And it makes me happy.
- Doing a big year is easy to measure. If you see a new species, it counts as one tick whether it is rare or common.
- Doing a big year requires planning, logistics, studying, and luck. These all take thought time, which leaves less time for negative thoughts.
- Every day has purpose. You wake up thinking, "How can I see more birds? Where should I go?"

We live in a fast-paced world. Just when we think things can't become any more complex, they do. Sometimes it feels as if one doesn't even have time to take a breath, let alone be able to enjoy some nonessential hobby like birding.

But life doesn't always play by our set of rules. It's popular to believe that the harder you work at something, the more you will achieve. And the more you achieve, the more money you'll make. The more money you make, the more things you can buy. The more you have, the happier you will be.

Is that really true? There is a satisfaction in owning things, but it is only short-lived. The truth is that the more things you own, the more things wear out, break down, and quit working. And if you own enough things you will find that, at some point, you run out of time to use them all. The things you worked so hard to acquire just sit in a corner, ignored, and your world becomes even more cluttered. Cares can layer on each other, distorting the heart's view like a magnifying glass. Once a person becomes overwhelmed, every problem looms larger than it really is.

You don't have to make a yearlong commitment like I did. Any birding can bring you soul-satisfying contentment. And while birding won't fix your problems, it is like Windex for the soul. It scrubs the window of your heart so you can see more clearly. It will give you a new perspective. And any help can make a difference. So try birding. Your life might change!

TIPS

- Choose something about birding that truly interests you. It doesn't have to be a competitive big year. The most important thing is that you enjoy it so much that it totally grabs your focus.
- Set aside time on your calendar to treat yourself regularly.
- Allow yourself to enjoy your activity with as few connections to everyday life as possible.
- Document your activities. Take pictures of yourself having fun. Keep a journal.
- Are you feeling depressed? Try looking at your pictures and reading your journal. It may just brighten your dark times as it did for me!

GREG MILLER has been enjoying birds and birding for more than fifty years. He is currently a tour guide with Wildside Nature Tours. He is also a speaker and personal guide for Greg Miller Birding.

Why I Love to Draw Birds

by Sophie Webb

FOR ME, BIRDS, ART, TRAVEL, AND BIOLOGY ARE INEXTRICABLY intertwined. My mother was an artist, the New England sculptor Nancy Webb. I blame her for my need to draw and create. Although her art as the years went by became more and more abstract, her muse was nature—the forms of bones, broken beetles, dried flowers, and pods. My earliest memories are with her, digging for earthworms in the garden and exploring the tidal wrack on the beaches of Cape Cod.

As a child, I was obsessed with animals of all kinds, and writing and drawing stories about them, so in the summers my parents sent me to Audubon camp, where I could explore some of those interests. Christmas and birthdays brought books such as *Songbirds in Your Garden* and *Birds of Prey of the World.* I was captivated by photos in the latter book of king vultures and crested caracaras, and I copied those pictures time and time again. We made numerous trips to the Peabody Museum at Harvard to look at the taxidermy mounts. Everything interested me, but I was particularly fascinated by a male frigatebird, with its huge red inflated gular pouch. Later in the Galapagos I remember being (stupidly) surprised by how soft, wobbly, and balloonlike the real pouch was, not hard plaster like on the mount of my childhood.

Although I loved drawing, art school didn't feel right for me, so after a year I transferred into a biology program, perhaps a better fit. Soon after graduating, I left the East Coast, sketchbook in hand, backpack on my back, and field projects in my future.

And so began years of travel, field projects, and sketchbooks. One thing I noticed very early was that when I draw a bird I look at it entirely differently than when I try to simply (or not so simply) identify it. There is some switch in my brain that—through the process of looking and putting the image on paper—causes me to learn more about the bird than when I just watch it, even if I am trying to study it carefully. Field sketching allows me to explore how a bird moves, its habits and structure, in an almost internal way. I can't quite say that once I have drawn a bird I will never forget it, particularly as I get older and my memory gets far less reliable, but it's close to being true.

All those field notebooks from travel and field projects have become my memories. When I look through the years' worth of books filled with drawings, images flood back—of where I saw each bird, and not only what it was doing, but why I was there, what the weather was like, and my mood.

There are pictures rendered the first day at 15,000 feet in the Andes, when I was suffering from *soroche,* altitude sickness, and unable to concentrate—my drawings of flamingoes simple like a child's, the line uncertain. In Amazonian Ecuador I drew duetting ocellated poorwills in the evening while slapping at mosquitos, and a roosting long-tailed potoo during the heat and humidity of day. These were detailed sketches of birds that remained mostly stationary for hours. Also in my notebooks are pages and pages of flight diagrams of seabirds, an obsession; intricate portraits of birds on nests from when I worked in the Galapagos; funny sketches of penguin antics and their chicks done while working in the Antarctic; studies from the Australian Museum where I visited after working on a field project studying bowerbirds; and drawings rendered while working for two and a half months on a Japanese stern trawler in the Gulf of Alaska. I think at times drawing was the only thing that kept me sane on that trip, as I was the sole English speaker and female on the ship.

There are times when I'm drawing in the forest and, by standing still for long periods, I believe I become invisible, allowing for wonderful prolonged views of some more secretive birds, such as a scaled antpitta or a noble antthrush slowly making its way down a trail. Many times, when I'm focusing on one bird, another will appear. I'll never forget such an incident in Chile: I was peering into a tangle of bamboo, searching for a huet-huet, a large species of tapaculo. I had started to sketch when a second bird, a chucao tapaculo, hopped up behind me and let loose with its impossibly loud gobbling call, surprising me so much that my sketchbook flew out of my hands, which, of course, startled the bird into scurrying back to its bamboo thicket.

When I lived in West Marin, a pair of fairly easy-to-find northern spotted owls lived out along the edge of Tomales Bay in a patch of old-growth oaks. So one afternoon I went out with my pad and pencil to find one to draw. I adore night birds, and any opportunity to draw an owl or nightjar from life is not to be missed. After a bit of searching, I found, not far up in an oak, a snoozing owl. A lazy eyelid opened slightly at my approach, a ruffle of feathers, and then back asleep. I sat down not far away and started to draw. Suddenly alert, the owl flew right over my head, landed briefly, and returned only seconds later to its original perch, a dusky-footed woodrat dangling from its talons!

On my travels I have found art and drawing can also educate people and cross cultural boundaries. One five-month trip Steve Howell and I took while working on *A Guide to the Birds of Mexico and Northern Central America* found us down in Honduras in our little VW Rabbit. It was the late 1980s, so parts of Central America were still feeling the repercussions of conflict. In Honduras every town seemed to have a military checkpoint, which slowed our days of travel greatly. It was a bit unnerving having to continuously get out of the car, explain why we were there, and show the young soldiers—who had large automatic rifles casually slung over their shoulders—our binoculars and field guides to prove to them what we were doing. I discovered, however, that as soon as I showed them my sketchbooks, broad smiles would appear on their faces and they would exclaim, "Ah, *carpintero*" (woodpecker), "*gavilán*" (hawk), or "*garza*" (heron). All tension was dispelled and we had a bond over a mutual admiration of their birds and my ability to sketch them.

These are some of the many reasons I love to draw birds: it has enhanced my travel, enriched the biology projects I have worked on, and given me hours of unutterable pleasure getting to know birds better through my pencil and paints. I have been fortunate to be able to build a career around birds, combining my interests in art and the natural world.

TIPS

This is my method; it may work for you, too.

- Though awkward to carry in the field, I frequently use a nine-by-twelve-inch pad and some sort of mechanical pencil.
- I first watch the bird for as long as it is readily in view.
- Then I do a gesture or multiple drawings of the whole bird to capture movement and proportion (hence the larger pad).
- I refine the drawing, often after again locating the bird.

- Finally, I add color. I use a small watercolor kit, but colored pencils work well and are handy in the field.

SOPHIE WEBB has traveled from the Antarctic to the Arctic to both draw and study birds. She is coauthor and illustrator of *A Guide to the Birds of Mexico and Northern Central America* and the *Field Guide to Marine Mammals of the Pacific Coast.* She is also the author-illustrator of three children's books about research projects she worked on. She is a director of Oikonos Ecosystem Knowledge and a research associate at Point Blue.

The Joy of Failure

by Richard Crossley

I'M NEVER HAPPIER THAN WHEN I'M OUTSIDE AND AT ONE with nature. A sunrise, a pattern of beautiful colors, something rare—these things amaze me. In fact, there's something great in just about everything if you view it with open eyes and see the wonder.

It seems like it should be a simple thing to get everyone to look at things this way, but it's not. Most people take nature for granted. It's something to be experienced on vacation, perhaps, but nature's spiritual sustenance isn't a daily need. Why does this happen? Perhaps people feel unable to appreciate nature because they think it requires expertise.

I feel very lucky about my upbringing. Much of my childhood was spent on farms. My dad, not a birder, was a countryside lover who marveled at the beauty of rolling fields, and he was never happier than when he was with his livestock, particularly cows. He was always pointing at things, getting my siblings and me to look closer.

I started hunting for eggs when I was seven. At age ten,

I switched to hunting for birds in my local area. Luckily enough, I was quite a serious birder by my early teens. When I was fifteen, I met some similarly aged birders who were traveling the country and chasing rarities, so I did that. In England, you had to take field notes and learn your craft. If you wanted to be one of the team, this is what you did—and I wanted to be one of them. (Peer pressure can be a wonderful thing!) By the time I was eighteen, I was starting to hunt for birds globally, following the lead of those before me. I fell in love with Cape May, New Jersey, during those travel times and settled here for good in 1991.

Since then, I've become an obsessed photographer and bird ID guide author, and I got caught up in lots of other things, too, mostly to do with my view of nature. As I get older and look back, I realize that while all of these activities involve birds, they are not really all about birding. What they all are is a license to be outside with nature; to look closely; to fill in the pieces of a puzzle, if you like.

There is an irony to doing puzzles. Does the enjoyment come from doing the puzzle, or finishing it? Yes, there is some satisfaction in accomplishing something, in taking it to a conclusion. Like putting a name on a bird: you can watch it for a few seconds, tick it, put it in a box, and then go home. But isn't that like completing a four-piece puzzle? Where is the fun? More importantly, where is the discovery?

Hunting for and finding the pieces of the puzzle are the

real fun. As an obsessive observer of birds and of the countryside in general, I appreciate that when I was young, I was encouraged to look and learn. There was nobody walking me around, telling me all the answers. It didn't take me long to realize that a bird's size, shape, behavior, and color patterns are all directly linked to one thing: the place where it lives. Once you understand the gravity of that statement, everything changes. Please think about that one. I will get back to it later.

We (humans, that is) are funny things. Most of us like to know what we are doing and to be good at the things we do. We don't like failure, right?

Birding is tough. There are thousands of species. They flit all over the place. They always seem to be hiding. They are so hard to see and so far away. You try, and then you try again, and then again. Each time: "No—nearly. No, it's too hard." A friend or a guide calls out the name. Of course, everyone else seems like an expert to you.

Too often, when we try something a few times—like assigning a name to a bird—but can't do it, we feel like a failure. Our defense mechanism for this is to stop doing it. It solves the problem—and so we stop looking and discovering.

But when we look closely, there is no right or wrong, no failure—just the enjoyment of discovering new things.

So back to size, shape, behavior, and a color pattern all being directly linked to where a bird, or any other animal, lives. If you think about this statement every day when you are outdoors, you will start to see incredible patterns. There is a reason for just about everything that happens in nature. Discovering those reasons is one of the most rewarding things in life. They are all around us, if we learn to see them.

This is much harder than it seems. Books and magazines have always fed us close-up photos of birds with fantastic feather details in out-of-focus backgrounds. Field guides show a bird's side profile against a white background, with two or three arrows pointing to the answers. These were not, are not, and never will be the answer. If they were, you would be out there finding it easy to do.

The solution is to dump the books—yes, including the Crossley ID Guides. Look out into your garden and ask yourself the simple question, what do I see? Describe it in more detail than you have ever done before. Then ask another question, and another. You will never be wrong. You will see more than you had seen before. And this will create even more questions.

Now you have discovered the act of discovery. Everything changes when this happens, not only for you, but for our future generations.

TIPS
- Look closely.
- Don't worry about being right or wrong—just enjoy the experience of discovery.

- Keep asking questions.

RICHARD CROSSLEY, as his essay suggests, lives a colorful life that is constantly changing. A recent trip through Europe forced him to reflect on his own views and what we can learn from others. He is the author of numerous books on birds, including The Crossley ID Guides.

Seabirding
HEADING INTO THE DEEP

by Alvaro Jaramillo

I LIKE THE SEA. I REALLY, REALLY LIKE THE SEA, ITS BIRDS AND whales, and all it has to offer. Yet I admit that while I enjoy the ocean, it often is a bit uncomfortable. Boats toss around, sometimes more than others; it can be wet and misty, and the days are long—sometimes really long! I often come back from a pelagic trip feeling like I have been out on the dance floor for five hours straight—tired, hungry, and thinking, "That hurt, but it was a ton of fun."

The birding adrenalin moments are more common on the ocean than on land. Birds can appear out of nowhere—seabirds are incredibly fast and travel huge distances, and they get lost or show up where they are not supposed to be. That is always great. They sometimes shoot in, for seconds that stretch out to minutes; they can reveal themselves in amazing clarity and gorgeousness before they disappear into nothing—poof! Petrels, albatrosses, puffins, murrelets, phalaropes, kittiwakes, storm-petrels, fulmars, shearwaters, or guillemots appear and make a birding day. Sometimes a rarity on the wrong side of the world can change a boat trip from a commonplace outing to the trip of the century. It all happens so fast and unpredictably.

It also can't be engineered—you flip a coin, you go out, and you see what decides to show itself to you. The chance of connection seems so small. The ocean is huge, the boat is tiny, and, although we think our prowess in observation is sizable, we really are detecting only a small radius around the boat, and sometimes very spottily, depending on the weather. So those chance events become very special.

The awkwardness of being out on a boat looking for birds is not lost on me, and it is part of what makes it fun. On land I can walk right up to the tree where a bird is singing, or I can pish to get a bird out of the bush—I am in my element as much as the bird is. On the ocean, I am out of my element. I am an intruder into a magical world, and I feel lucky to see it over and over again. Whales, dolphins, fur seals, sharks, jellyfish, Mola mola, tuna, sargassum weed, turtles—the other players out there are as fun as the birds are, and equally special. There are few enough of them at sea that they make their mark, they become part of the birding, unlike what happens on land. There, you may see hundreds of species of plants, a few mammals, tens or even hundreds of insects, and, unless you are a naturalist of the highest caliber, you can't keep track of it all. But on a boat trip, each creature counts and can be enjoyed in a more leisurely way. Sometimes a rare dolphin or whale, or a great white shark, can be the "bird" of the day. The ocean excites me, makes me feel alive, gets my veins pumping.

With all I have described, it may seem insurmountable to know what everything is—and how do you even gain experience in a place that you so seldom visit? The key to ocean voyages, particularly for the newbie, is preparation. There are not that many species out there, but all are different from what is on land. Look at imagery, books, and even the abundance charts on eBird to determine what they look like and how regularly occurring each one of them is. Also clarify in your mind what a shearwater is, a storm-petrel, an albatross, and so on. Know the groups, so that when someone yells, "*Pterodroma* petrel at three o'clock," you will at least have a reasonable expectation of what you will see. Being prepared—getting primed—works wonders on your birding, particularly when visiting a place that you do not know well. You will miss out if you are unprepared. I love the challenge and excitement of pre-tour preparations—wondering what oddity or rarity may, could, one day might show up.

Birding is rich and deep, and goes beyond just names of birds, molt patterns, and the beauty of birds. I try to give new birders the advice to let the emotional and deep side of birding permeate them, to allow it to be the life-changing type

of experience that it has the potential to be. In addition, for me, seabirding connects my birding to my family and even to who I am.

With that in mind, let me take you back to my first experience on the ocean. I was about seven or eight years old in Chile. The sun had just set on the port of Puerto Montt, and we were off on a large wooden skiff with an outboard motor. We were to motor all night to a fjord inside of Chiloé Island to visit the *Halcón Rojo II,* a refurbished U.S. World War II minesweeper, one of the first large fishing boats in Chile. I was there with my dad and crew. It started well and got even better for me as I fell asleep quickly in the lulling movement of the boat on the water and the white noise of that old engine. But morning made my heart quicken—we had shipwrecked! The sailor had gone too close to one of many islets on Chiloé, and our propeller was broken.

For a little kid, this was all fun. The islet had a single house, where we were taken in, and I had my first ever *chapaleles,* a potato bread that has more in common with a rubber tire than real food. But at least I wasn't hungry. The kids in the house stared at me intently; maybe I was the first city kid they had ever seen. Before the day had passed, we were rescued and towed to the *Halcón Rojo II,* which translates to the *Red Falcon.*

The *Halcón Rojo* was no random boat—this was my Un-

cle Alfonso's boat. My uncle was a legend. He took the first
Halcón Rojo, a tiny vessel with only one other crew member,
clear across the ocean from Chile to Tahiti. There he became
a crew member on the *Wanderer,* the tall ship owned by Hollywood actor and adventurer Sterling Hayden. He eventually
ended up in Sausalito, California, where he picked up the
Halcón Rojo II cheap in the early 1960s, and then brought his
most trusted engineer to help him refurbish this vessel as a
modern fishing boat. That engineer was my dad.

There is much more to say about the *Halcón Rojo II* and
its history; in fact, books have been written about it. I did not
live this history, but I did set foot on that boat, fished from
that boat, and enjoyed nature from that boat. My dad and his
brother built boats for fun as kids, on a lake in Chile—they
have boats and water in their blood. Now, as an adult, I realize that for me, pelagic trips are more than birding; they are
my connection to my family history. But then, isn't birding
often more than just birding? Discovery, adventure, that salty
tinge on the lips connects me to my family. I think about
the fact that my dad and my uncle likely saw Nazca boobies,
pink-footed shearwaters, black-footed albatross, and all sorts
of goodies on their trips, even if they didn't know what they
were. I have heard stories from these guys about fjords with
caves full of whale bones, big fish caught on the line, and long
trips down the Pacific Coast.

Birding on the ocean is deeply meaningful for me because

of the beauty of what is out there, the excitement of finding new things, and the adventure. I am not a spiritual guy, but out there I can't help but feel my past looking down at me and smiling, because the ocean is still in our blood and I am there to represent.

TIPS

- Prime yourself for what is coming. There is nothing like preparation, whether reviewing warbler songs before they return in spring, or looking at guides and imagery of common seabirds before your first pelagic trip.
- Expect the expected. Even in pelagic birding, where abundance and distribution of the birds change offshore every day, there are birds that are more common, and those that are uncommon. Looking at status, such as eBird bar charts, helps to whittle down the possibilities when tackling a new area.
- Birding is a life-changing experience, spiritual even. Allow birding to become this—open yourself up to the emotions, community, aesthetics, and friendships that develop while enjoying feathered creatures. It can be so enriching!

ALVARO JARAMILLO is a lifelong birder, biologist, and writer. He is the author of *Birds of Chile* and the new *American Birding Association Field Guide to Birds of California*.

He is involved in various projects from conservation and birding in Colombia to understanding the molecular history of vermilion flycatcher. He runs international birding tours and pelagic trips with his company, Alvaro's Adventures, in Half Moon Bay, California.

Museums

Donna L. Dittmann

THROUGHOUT MY LONG BIRDING CAREER I HAVE USED museum collections extensively to investigate various questions I found unanswered by field guides. It started at California Academy of Sciences (CAS). After a how-to-handle-specimens tutorial, then Curator of Ornithology Dr. Laurence C. Binford turned me loose to explore the contents of the specimen cabinets at CAS. It was 1972, and to a fifteen-year-old interested in birds, this was an amazing world. Drawer after drawer, species upon species, I envisioned questions answered.

The unidentifiable *Empidonax*: my Golden Guide indicated the prudent course was simply to not attempt to identify non-breeding or silent individuals. My Peterson Field Guide stated, "collecting has proven that it is nearly impossible to name many indiviculals in the field." However, *these specimens* were positively identified in their trays. So how could I translate the appearance of the specimens to field identification? There must be a way, I thought. I could see differences, yes—subtle

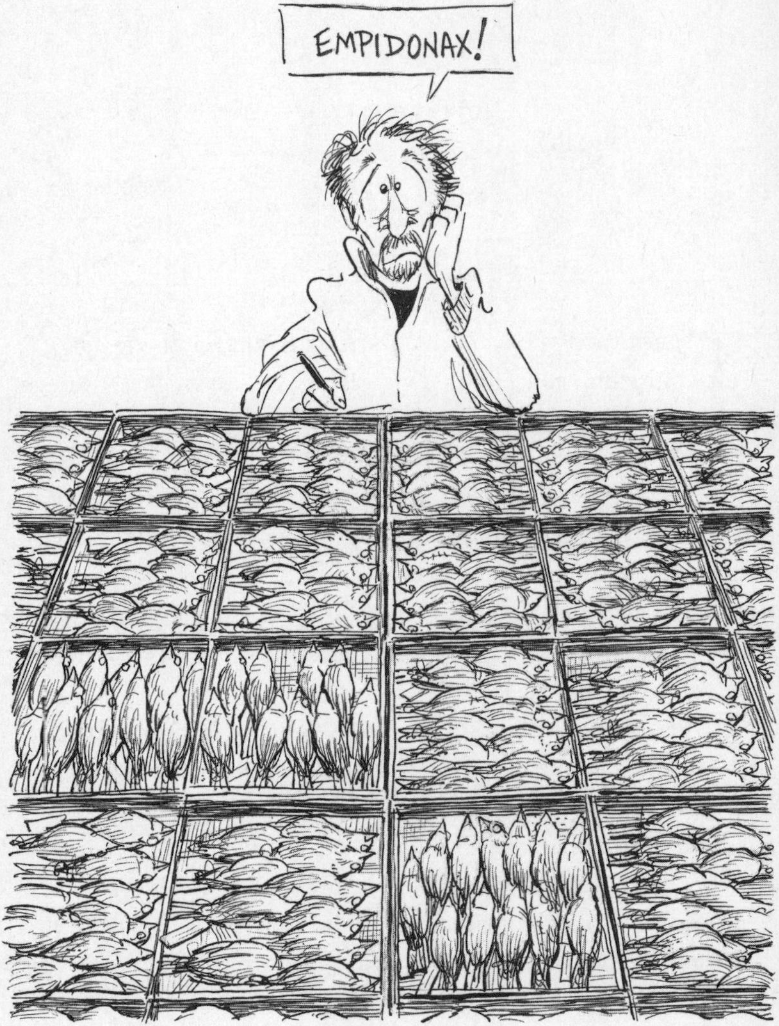
EMPIDONAX!

color differences of olive and yellow, the pattern of the outer webs of the rectrices, whether the plumage was worn or fresh, and structural details of the size and shape of the bill. I would visit these same drawers many times in the future.

This was the beginning of my love affair with museum specimens. There were ooh-ah moments: exploring the amazing diversity of birds represented in the collection, being able to touch a bird of paradise, smell pungent Procellariiformes when their cabinet was breached, and see up close countless species I had not yet encountered. Many of my visits were to investigate specific questions not answered in my field guides, such as plumage differences between fresh fall grasshopper and Le Conte's sparrows, variation in fall plumages of warblers, and bill differences between sooty and short-tailed shearwaters. Plus, I could make sketches of specimens—stationary birds—ultimately improving my ability to draw live birds.

As a more "advanced" birder, I embarked on an adventure with birding friends Hank and Priscilla Brodkin. Destination: Peru. Alas, we had no Peru field guide—only de Schauensee, which covered *all* of South America, and *Birds of Venezuela*, both already in my book collection. I created my own Peru guide with colored-pencil sketches of species I thought we might encounter, which ended up being less than useful. During the trip I could identify *some* of the obvious species we saw. Others I sketched, hoping to be able to key them out in the future. Many fleeting glimpses or more cryptic species were simply left unidentified. Bottom line—the tropics were humbling.

In 1982, I combined a birding trip to Louisiana with a visit to the LSU Museum of Natural Science (LSUMNS), which included recent collections from Peru. Despite being a regular at CAS, I nonetheless received basic instruction on how to use the collection from Curator of Ornithology Dr. J. V. Remsen, who proudly directed my attention to data-rich labels on recently collected specimens. Recorded data provide insights to a bird's age or breeding condition: skull ossification, presence of a bursa of Fabricius, condition of gonads (including whether a female's oviduct is straight or convoluted), and so on. Modern data have significantly assisted in-hand identification treatises aimed at bird banders (such as Peter Pyle's indispensable manual). These detailed guides provide a wealth of information for more advanced birders.

Over the next few days, I was allowed to pursue answers to my many questions in the bird range. There were successes: when I searched trays of spinetail species, my field sketch of the lovely mystery spinetail (the one with the creamy white crown) matched specimens of *Cranioleuca albicapilla* (creamy-crested spinetail).

I was also able to make sketches of specimens for future reference, and simply browse their holdings. Of course, there was an added bonus: I could see species recently discovered

Donna L. Dittmann

by LSUMNS personnel that were not yet even illustrated in field guides (such as long-whiskered owlet) and meet some of the ornithologists who had discovered them, such as Dr. John P. O'Neill. And I did get to go birding, including with LSUMNS graduate students.

In 1983, I embarked on my next Peru trip as a member of a three-month LSUMNS expedition to assist with an investigation of species' genetic differences across Amazonian rivers. Before departure, I learned how to prepare scientific specimens so I could contribute, a privilege and skill that also greatly enhanced my abilities as a birder. The trip also added to my appreciation of the arduous work invested in collections. A specimen can take anywhere from forty-five minutes to several hours to prepare, depending on size or other factors. Many collections are made in very remote areas. In the steamy

Amazon rainforest, I lived in a tent, ate tuna and noodles, and drank from and bathed in a stream; we were two days by boat from the nearest city and, back in those days, without phone or radio contact.

Field guides have improved vastly since my first museum visit in 1972, and museum collections have contributed to the knowledge and detailed illustrations contained between their covers. Various authors have discussed the broad utility of research specimens, including many applications relevant to birders. Museum collections are not antiquated "stamp collections," but instead active repositories of biodiversity. Even older specimens that predate modern label data and tissue samples continue to unravel secrets. The research value of scientific specimens will only increase in the future. Studies routine today were not imagined when I browsed the collection at CAS over forty years ago, and there is always something new that can be learned.

I often wondered why more birders didn't take advantage of museum collections as a resource. How does a birder access the cloistered contents of a research collection? Many museums host public events and open their doors to the public during open houses that include tours of their research collections. My introduction to a museum research collection followed a student ornithology course offered at CAS. Many museums offer similar courses and seminars aimed at adults and children. But if you would like to investigate a specific question, contact the museum's ornithology curator, introduce yourself and your interests, and ask if you can schedule a visit. Many museums accept volunteers, which is also an excellent way to get hands-on experience: I was a volunteer in various capacities at CAS, San Bernardino County Museum, and LSUMNS before being hired as the specimen preparator and collection manager for the LSUMNS Section of Genetics Resources.

TIPS

Here are some fun websites to check out for help with bird identification:

- https://www.fws.gov/lab/featheratlas/idfeather.php
- http://collections.nmnh.si.edu/search/birds/
- http://www.pugetsound.edu/academics/academic-resources/slater-museum/biodiversity-resources/birds/wing-image-collection/

DONNA DITTMANN is a collections manager and preparator at the Louisiana State University Museum of Natural Science. She has prepared over 11,000 specimens archived in museum collections all over the world. She is active with public outreach, especially the birding community, and helped create and coordinates the agritourism event Yellow Rails and Rice Festival. She is also an artist who combines birding and photography skills with artistic design and digital technology.

Being a Bird Guide in Panama
Is the Best Job Ever!

by Carlos A. Bethancourt

BIRD WATCHING IS AMAZING. I LOVE EVERY ASPECT OF IT, from calls and colors to interesting behavior. I love that while I am birding I can connect with the natural world as well as with other birders.

"Look, look, look, everyone get on this bird, to the left of the laser. It's a nice rufous motmot—and close! Scope view! Notice how it is different from the broad-billed we saw earlier, with the rufous color extending to the belly; it is way longer, and no green on the throat. Watch how it wags its tail from side to side like a pendulum. This thing is huge! Did everyone get a good look? Great! Anyone need a digiscope? What a fantastic bird—this is going to be a great morning. Listen . . . you hear that? . . . Leaves rustling like it's raining? Ants ahead, and a whole bunch of birds!"

This is a typical morning for me, guiding tours along Semaphore Hill, just down from the Canopy Tower. And though the motmot is an old friend, and I don't experience the rush of an actual lifer, when I see the joy and delight on the faces of the birders—some first-timers to the Neotropics—I often think back to my first sighting of that species, and it's nearly as exhilarating for me as if it were *my* lifer as well. My excitement is in the sharing.

During our afternoon of birding we see a small, close-up, mixed flock: red-legged honeycreeper with golden-hooded, plain, and blue-gray tanagers, among a few others. I tell the folks to check out the colors on these birds; in the nice light, they almost glow. I often hear from birders that they have seen plenty of blue-grays but never took the time to really look at the colors, and that if I hadn't gotten so excited, they probably would have just passed them by. I also hear, "What got you so fascinated with birding?"

So I tell them about a very special person from almost twenty-eight years ago, and one of the birds we just saw. I grew up in the small village of Huile (pronounced "willy") that borders the western end of the old Canal Zone. Back then, the forest was all around us, and as a nine-year-old I was not immune to a little mischief. One typical day, I was out with my slingshot looking for things to shoot, when I saw a bunch of birds. I took aim, shot, and, to my amazement, a bird fell to the ground. I was so proud; I was a great hunter! I confidently took the bird to the special person and showed it to her, just knowing she would be glad for me.

Well, not exactly. She asked if I felt happy about this.

"*Yes!*" I answered.

She then casually asked, "How do you want it?"

"Want it? You mean eat it? I don't want to eat it."

She replied, "Then why did you kill it?"

I had simply wanted to shoot something with my slingshot.

It was only then that I noticed its beautiful colors: the different shades of brilliant blue, the black on the wings with yellow underneath, with a splash of aqua on the crown. And, of course, the bright red legs. I later found out, as you have probably guessed, that it was a red-legged honeycreeper. Every time I see one, I think back to that pivotal moment that shaped my life. That was the day I began to appreciate and respect nature, especially birds. That was when I started looking at birds as something to study, admire, and enjoy. And I owe it all to a very special person, my grandma, Graciela Martinez, who, at ninety-eight, still lives happily in a modest house on the edge of the forest in Huile.

Guiding for the past fifteen years has given me the opportunity to work with many birding professionals who have become my dear friends. I look forward to seeing them at festivals, where we can swap birding stories and catch up. I meet lots of other people at festivals, too, and talk with them about birding in Panama. Many visit our booth for several years before making the decision to travel, and it is great to finally see them in Panama and share our birds and other wildlife with them. I love to hear them say, "Carlos, I don't know why I waited so long to visit!" This job has allowed me to meet birders from all over the world. I have stayed in contact with most of them over the years. Quite a few have returned to bird Panama a second time, and some even more. It is great to know that so many people love birding in Panama as much as I do. The challenge of getting target (or "wish-list") birds for clients keeps me on my toes and makes for exciting birding. My birding friendships have also led me to bird in other countries, and even on other continents, like Africa.

Life teaches us many good lessons. The honeycreeper I shot with my slingshot so many years ago changed my life in many good ways. It led me to bird watching, and today that's how I make my living and support my family. Yes, being a bird guide in Panama is the best job ever!

TIPS
- Remember, Neotropical birding can sometimes be challenging. You may not see all the birds the guide or others in the group see, nor will you always get that "field guide" view. Don't be disappointed if you miss one or two. There will be plenty of birds to check on your list each night, and the ones you miss give you a great reason to come back for a second try!
- Even though your guide will know the birds and their calls, it is helpful to study the possible species before

your trip; this will be especially useful for when you come upon a mixed flock or do some birding on your own between outings. I have found that some birders like the challenge of making IDs on their own, making the memory of that bird even more special—but they still want the reassurance of my confirming nod.

CARLOS A. BETHANCOURT was born in Panama City in 1978 and raised in the small village of Huile. After high school, Carlos attended Mt. Hood Community College in Oregon, where he received his first training in ornithology. Carlos began his guiding career in 2000 with the Canopy Family and enjoys spending time with his wife, Evelyn, and their two kids, Cristy and Roberto Carlos.

Why I Love Being a
Self-proclaimed Bird Evangelist

by Ann Nightingale

ACCORDING TO THE DICTIONARY, AN EVANGELIST IS A person who talks about something with great enthusiasm. That just about sums me up these days when it comes to anything about birds. It wasn't always that way. Once I was converted, though, let's just say my enthusiasm could reasonably be mistaken for religious fervor.

In the scheme of things, I was a latecomer to birding, taking up the hobby seriously when I was forty. Not being able to identify birds was one of my life regrets (the other being not knowing the constellations). I'd bought field guides, had an old pair of binoculars, and could recognize most of the common backyard birds, but when it came to the little brown jobs, I was lost and alone in the wilderness.

In 1996, I had the good fortune to work with my soon-to-become birding mentor, Alan MacLeod. He took a group of birding neophytes out with the promise that he would "knock our socks off." He did. Alan was naming birds left, right, and center, and without even seeing them. He was identifying the birds *by their songs!* I didn't even know this was possible.

Over the next year, I pored over local field guides and checklists, and listened to bird songs and training lectures on CD, and by spring I was able to identify most of the local birds visually and by song. Amazing! I was hooked, and hooked well. Admittedly, shorebirds and gulls can still take me back twenty years, but once I could give the birds names, the conversion was underway.

Soon after, on a visit to a bird banding station, Rocky Point Bird Observatory, I watched as volunteers weighed and measured a fox sparrow. They had captured this very same bird for five consecutive years. I was awestruck. This bird passed through the same hundred-yard-wide strip of land every year for at least five years! This was not just "a" fox sparrow— this was an individual with a connection to this specific place. Perhaps because of their capacity for flight and their long-distance migrations, I had always thought of birds as extremely mobile and ephemeral. All of a sudden, my mind was flooded with the thoughts of how changes in *this* habitat could disorient or even displace these birds from their homes or migration routes. How could it be that we'd never been taught about this? I felt an overwhelming responsibility to spread the word!

Over the next few years I absorbed every birdy fact I found, like three-year-olds absorb every curse word they hear. The more I learned, the more I knew I didn't know. And not only didn't *I* know, but hardly anyone I knew knew. I guess I'd always figured that since humans had been in the company of birds "forever," we probably had already discovered just about everything there was to learn about them. I was wrong, so very wrong. The more I saw, read, and heard, the more I felt compelled to share abundant ornitho-trivia with everyone I met.

I have regaled garden club members with dos and don'ts of attracting birds to their gardens, wowed my friends with the longevity records of tiny hummingbirds and wrens, shared migration stories of individuals banded in one location being recaptured in another thousands of miles away year after year, and opened people's ears to learning how to tell birds apart just by their songs and vocalizations.

And the most surprising thing of all? Almost everyone I've met is as excited as I am to know more about our feathered friends! This is a knowledge gap so many people have, and there is truly a hunger to know more. Just in time, too, I hope. Humans have been amazingly effective at creating hazards for birds and, for the most part, are completely unaware how their actions can have negative effects.

If there is one theme that I can single out that causes folks to stop, think, and in some cases change their ways, it is the same one that got to me: site loyalty. Whenever I tell people that the birds in their yard this year are some of the very same ones that were there last year, I see a transformation. These familiar strangers, whose names they may not know, instantly change from anonymous visitors to friends and neighbors, or even family.

And then the stories come: the time the hummingbirds arrived and stared in the window when the feeder wasn't up; the bird that keeps getting stuck in the garage; the chickadee that perches nearby, making a fuss while the seeds are being topped up; the robin that comes down every time they weed the garden; the birdhouse that was occupied for years, then all of a sudden wasn't. Almost everyone has a personal story that suddenly makes sense when they realize that they are literally sharing their space with specific individuals, not just random birds.

Evangelists often speak of salvation. I fervently believe that once people learn about birds, they will want to save them. If we can save the birds, maybe we can even save the planet. That very prospect is why I love being a self-proclaimed bird evangelist. Can I get an "amen"?

TIPS

We all have a part to play in this avian evangelical movement.

- *Learn who your neighbors are.* Kenn Kaufman said in a 2007 interview with *Birding* magazine, "My wish is that every person might learn to recognize fifty species of plants and animals native to his or her own region. That basic level of natural history could revolutionize our view of humanity's place in the world." That connection, that little something that makes a tree, a butterfly, or a bird personal, is what changes everything.

• *Love your neighbors.* We are still learning how birds are loyal not only to their breeding grounds, but also to their wintering grounds, and to the routes they travel between them. If we want to protect our birds, we need to know what's happening to them when they are out of our sight, too, opening our minds to the need for global conservation efforts. Take care of your birds by being good stewards of your shared lands, providing good food and water, keeping them safe at home, and helping conserve their more distant destinations.

• *Talk to your neighbors—the human ones.* If you learn a little about the birds in your area, you will know more than most of the people in your community. Spend time with other birders and share what you learn with others.

A NN NIGHTINGALE is an avid birder, field trip leader, and amateur naturalist from Vancouver Island, Canada. She volunteers for Rocky Point Bird Observatory, the Victoria Natural History Society, and several other organizations, spreading the good news about birds and birding wherever she goes.

Urban Birding—
What's That All About?

by David Lindo

PHNOM PENH, CAMBODIA, 2009: RICKSHAWS BUSTLE, countless motorcycles buzz, the majestic French colonial buildings glow, boulevards wide and grand buckle with traffic, food markets throng with hungry urbanites. Hubbub— the typical scene in Cambodia's capital city.

Unbeknown to anyone, a species of bird completely new to science was hiding in plain sight. Routine mist netting of birds by ornithologists researching avian flu at a construction site at the edge of the city revealed an odd-looking tailorbird. Tailorbirds are members of the Old World warbler family so named because of the meticulous detail they get into when weaving their nests together. The captured bird was later discovered to be a new species, the Cambodian tailorbird (*Orthotomus chaktomuk*), sending shock waves among ornithologists around the world. Finding a new species for the world in the middle of nowhere is the accepted norm, but to find one in the middle of somewhere? What other amazing birds, rare or otherwise, await discovery right under our noses in our towns and cities?

"The only birds you see in cities are pigeons." This is one of the lines that people have fed me repeatedly throughout my life. The other is "You have to go into the countryside to see wildlife." When I was young, I almost believed them— almost. Today, I can understand why people still might think that. If your average day involves sitting, or more often standing, on a train or bus doing the journey to and from work with your head variously buried in newspapers, kindles, and iPads, or cupped in your hands as you grab the last possible moments for extra sleep, of course you are not going to notice much else around you. If you are strolling to school, the office, or the stores listening to music on your headphones, you are not going to hear much. If you gaze into store windows and never look up, then you will be bound to miss the swifts wafting on the breeze above your head like bits of burnt paper. If you go to the park only to use it as a shortcut, never stopping to watch a pollen-laden honeybee collecting nectar from the flowers that line your route, then you are missing out on a lot.

I remember one morning, several winters ago, following a flock of glorious bohemian waxwings that were feeding on rowan tree berries on Warren Street just off Tottenham Court Road, right in the heart of London. What surprised me most was not the fact that the flock of some two hundred birds chose such an inner-city site to indulge in their foraging. No, it was the commuters who successfully managed to walk with blinders on, staring straight ahead, past the trilling birds, some of which were dangling just inches above their heads. As these commuters powered on, hell-bent on getting to the office on time, they didn't even notice the small posse of birders gathered at the roadside in awe of those gorgeous northern wanderers.

I was born in west London, and I have always been fascinated by natural history. Indeed, from birth I had a general interest in anything animate, which is something that still burns within me to this day. I began to focus on birds by the time I was five, starting my urban birding life thereafter. It was when I was a teenager watching birds out in the countryside that I realized how rich urban birding really is. When nonbirders told me that proper birding could be conducted only outside of towns, it was clear to me this was a very shortsighted assumption, one that I have never understood. Birds actively seek the habitat that's available to them within our growing metropolises. The city provides a haven, albeit a sometimes fragile and temporary one. Very often it is a sanctuary that is forever under the omnipresent dark cloud of development.

Birds are everywhere. This is a phrase that I constantly repeat to everyone I meet. The notion that there are birds living among us in urban areas is by no means a recent thing. They have fluttered around us since the first hut was ever thatched, the first brick laid, the first parking meter anchored, and the first *X Factor* audition. My message is very simple: we all need to appreciate that wildlife not only occurs in our cities, but that it is here to stay. We need to be aware that this wildlife is all around us. We need to actively encourage this fabulous life and conserve the places in which it exists—urban or otherwise—whether by nurturing invertebrates within a tiny window box on the fifth-floor ledge of an apartment block, promoting small wild areas in our gardens, creating areas set aside for wildlife in our local parks, watching over a forgotten wild corner of our local neighborhood, or starting a green roof project. If we can learn about the importance of wildlife conservation in our cities, then we will understand its connection in the general web of life on this planet, enabling us to reach out and strive to protect the rest of the world's fauna and flora.

Urban birding is a great conduit through which to spread that message. As long as birds exist, there will still be hope.

TIPS
- Don't get hung up on trying to identify everything that moves. Take your time and soak up the experiences. Knowledge comes over time.
- Enjoy yourself.
- Keep looking up!

DAVID LINDO has written countless articles on urban birds for many websites and publications and is a regular television and radio presenter on the BBC as well as other channels around the world, including CBS in the United States. David is the author of *The Urban Birder* and *Tales from Concrete Jungles* and is a Fellow member of the International League of Conservation Writers and a member of the British Guild of Travel Writers. He is also a proud ambassador for Leica Birding and the London Wildlife Trust.

Why I Love Seabirds

by Debi Shearwater

WHEN I FELL FOR SEABIRDS, I FELL HARD. FOR SHEAR-waters. And albatrosses. And petrels. And storm-petrels. I didn't just "love" them. I fell in love with them.

There is something so mysterious and curious about birds that live their entire lives at sea, except for coming to land to breed. What do they eat? Where do they go? Why adopt that lifestyle? What are their predators? How do they navigate?

As a fledgling birder living in Texas in 1972, I had fallen in love with warblers at High Island. Colorful beyond imagination, forever on the move, these brightly colored gems enchanted me in my early birding days. After all, my very first field guide, *A Field Guide to the Birds of Texas* by Roger Tory Peterson, portrayed most birds in black-and-white illustrations. The warblers were shown in color. It was hard to get excited about shearwaters in black and white.

Nevertheless, a pivotal moment in my life occurred that year when I read the book *Shearwaters* by Ronald Lockley. His studies of the Manx shearwaters on the island of Skokholm captivated me. My Peterson Field Guide illustrated sooty and Audubon's shearwaters, in black and white, on page seven. Inclusion in the field guide almost appeared to be an afterthought for these birds. "Habitat: Open seas," it stated. Who goes birding on the open seas, I wondered?

A few years later, however, I found myself living in Monterey, California, where a magnetic attraction to the shearwaters empowered me to learn as much as possible about seabirds and their world. So I set out to do just that. Within a few months of arriving, I began to offer pelagic trips for birders every month of the year. When a rare streaked shearwater showed up on one of my early trips, I began to make trips available to birders throughout the United States, and eventually the world. Birders hoping to score new ticks for their list flew in from all parts of the country, forming a new birding community—the seabirders. We made discoveries. We set records. It was the heyday of seabirding. Many birders called seabirding the "last frontier" of birding. It may well be.

Forty years ago, scientists were just beginning to learn more about shearwaters, albatrosses, petrels, and stormpetrels. Indeed, even today, new discoveries are being made— witness Bryan's shearwater, a newly described species. Those black-and-white illustrations of decades ago have given way to the digital camera and countless new, colorful seabird field guides.

Every summer millions of sooty shearwaters arrive off the central coast of California from their breeding islands in New Zealand and Chile. They come to feed in the nutrient-rich waters of Monterey Bay, especially. Although this has long been known by scientists, only more recently with satellite tagging have the details of this remarkable trans-equatorial migration been revealed. Sooty shearwaters take advantage of the prevailing winds along different parts of the migration route, tracing giant figure eights over the Pacific basin. It was discovered that a sooty shearwater travels some 39,000 miles each year—the longest animal migration route ever recorded using electronic tracking technology. Sooty shearwaters live in an "eternal summer." What's not to like about that?

Food is not evenly distributed at sea. Certain areas are known to be productive, and Monterey Bay is one of the top five areas in the world. A deep submarine canyon bisects the bay. This canyon is as deep as the Grand Canyon. Indeed, one marine biologist said that if it weren't filled with water, we'd all be riding donkeys down into it. This canyon, in combination with our currents and prevailing winds, causes a phenomenon known as *upwelling,* which brings the cold, nutrient-rich waters to the surface, thereby feeding the entire food chain. It's all about food. I can't think of any other life zone that illustrates the entire food chain so well as the open ocean: krill feed on phytoplankton and are in turn fed on by everything from tiny Cassin's auklets to blue sharks and squid, to the largest animal on Earth, the blue whale.

It has been thrilling to be involved with seabirds—to learn so much and discover new records for North America. This work has led me to Antarctica, South Georgia, New Zealand, and many of the breeding islands of these magnificent seabirds. It gave me a sense of completion to have seen the shearwaters, albatrosses, petrels, and storm-petrels at their feeding areas and then at their nesting islands—as though somehow I had completed a "migration" of sorts.

Over the decades I have observed changes at sea—such as declining numbers of sooty shearwaters and ashy storm-petrels—which motivated me to work on seabird conservation. Seabirds have many threats: introduced predators at their breeding islands, including cats, rats, rabbits, goats, and mongoose; oil spills; fishery interactions; plastics and pollution; and habitat destruction. Of all the world's birds, seabirds are the most threatened group. Great strides have been made, but more needs to be accomplished.

From a drab black-and-white illustration of a shearwater to an explosion of new knowledge about seabirds and their world, it has been an all-consuming adventure. Ultimately, I didn't just fall in love with shearwaters—I fell in love with the *ocean*.

What about you? Are you ready to test the waters of the world of seabirds?

TIPS

- Look beyond the trees, marshes, and grasslands to the open ocean. More than 70 percent of Earth is covered with water. Isn't it time to test it out?
- Choose your trip wisely. Some marine areas are more productive than others.
- If you just cannot go to sea, become a seabird conservationist. The seabirds need you!

D EBI SHEARWATER is well known for establishing Shearwater Journeys, a company that has offered pelagic trips departing from California since 1976. Many seabird records new to North America have been found on her trips. More than 65,000 nature lovers have joined her at sea. She has witnessed many changes in marine life over more than four decades at Monterey Bay. Debi has visited all seven continents and countless remote islands where seabirds breed. She enthusiastically leads expedition voyages to these unique areas, including the Galapagos Islands, the Russian Far East, and Antarctica.

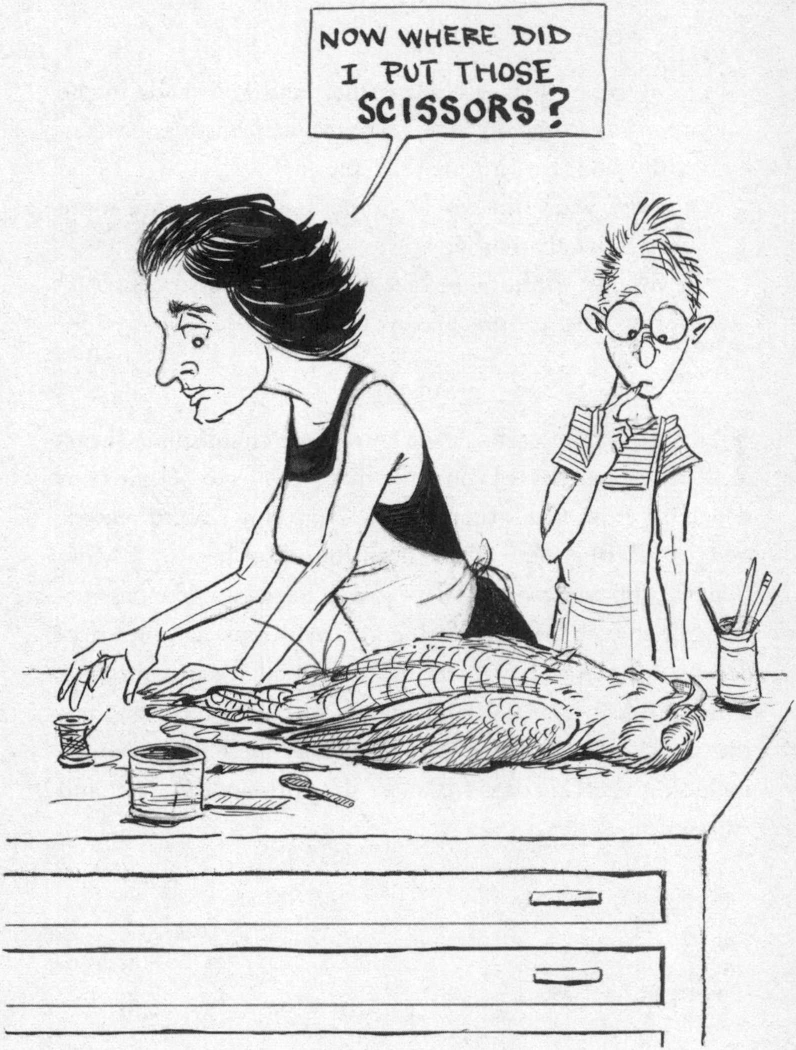
NOW WHERE DID I PUT THOSE SCISSORS?

More Than Skin Deep

Working in the Prep Lab at the Museum of Vertebrate Zoology

by Ioana Seritan

I HAVE LOVED BIRDS ALL MY LIFE, BUT IT TOOK ME A FEW years to realize birding existed. The moment I finished ninth grade, I borrowed my brother's binoculars and took a walk around my neighborhood. Before long, a tiny bird with a black vest and white trousers flitted out in front of me and back to a tree in someone's yard. From that very first sighting of a black phoebe, I fell deeply in love with wild birds. However, when I decided to attend the University of California–Berkeley and volunteer in the university's Museum of Vertebrate Zoology, I had no idea I would end up learning how to skin and stuff birds for the museum collection.

If you're surprised that a passionate bird-lover (and a vegetarian!) would dedicate herself to skinning birds, you are far from the first. My favorite response came from an old friend during brunch a couple of years ago. She leaned over the table, lowered her voice, and asked, "Don't you feel like that kind of thing attracts serial killers?" I know it can seem scary or creepy. But the reality is that skinning birds is an amazing learning experience.

I have loved watching birds in their natural habitats for years. Now I get to see and touch birds with my own hands, and apply what I learn from those individuals to birds that are still alive and singing. Skinning birds has taught me more about anatomy, morphology, and development than any other source. When I hear birds sing, I can reference what I know about syringes (the vocal organs of birds). When I hear an Anna's hummingbird dive and spread its tail to produce that famous high note, I can think about the hummingbird tail feathers I've observed. With every specimen I prepare, I learn more about birds, and about myself. For me, preparing specimens only increases the respect and wonder I feel for birds. I promise that when I look at wild birds, I see more than dancing drumsticks . . . unless I haven't eaten in a while.

Volunteering in a prep lab has taught me a vast amount, but it isn't good for only me. Museum collections are good for all of us who value the environment. By preserving animals that have died, we can continue telling their stories for hundreds of years. Every animal that enters a natural history museum is a repository of information. We collect as much data as we can during every preparation, because we have no idea what information researchers might want in the future. A century ago, no one could have imagined the kind of genetic research we conduct today. Now taking tissue samples for DNA extraction is standard protocol. Who knows what data or samples researchers might need a hundred years from now? We describe absolutely everything, just to be sure.

After we examine every inch of the bird, we put it back together again. A well-prepared and preserved specimen should last ages—with emphasis on *well*. There are not very many steps in the process of stuffing a bird, but those steps do take patience and artistry. The first step is to create new eyeballs out of cotton. After that, we wrap the end of a dowel in cotton to become the bird's new brain and backbone. Then we create a body out of cotton and sew the bird's skin gently around it.

My absolute favorite thing about skinning and stuffing birds is that it reminds me how enjoyable it is to learn. Skinning birds employs the most fun method of learning: sitting down and doing something badly a hundred times. For example, the first step of making a body—rolling new eyeballs— often takes me the longest. You might think that after rolling dozens of nice-looking eyeballs, I would be able to do it easily and quickly. You would be wrong. Most of the time, I have to spend half an hour relearning how to make a good sphere out of cotton. (That process teaches me a lot more than rolling spheres—it also teaches me how to roll cylinders and misshapen lumps.) Rolling eyeballs is a balm for my perfectionism. There is nothing more humbling than being bested by an inanimate pile of cotton. As frustrating as that is, it is even more exciting. Working in the museum gives me the chance to try, and fail, and try again. Being a specimen preparator has taught me one of my favorite lessons: I might not always have a clue what I'm doing, but I will eventually.

Having the opportunity to learn and volunteer in the Museum of Vertebrate Zoology's prep lab is a privilege. I am grateful for the chance to participate in the museum's long history of specimen preparation. My name is now preserved in the same cabinets as collectors and preparators before me, such as Joseph Grinnell, the first director of the museum. Grinnell and his team collected many specimens for the museum all over western North America. His meticulous records allow current preparators to conduct the Grinnell Resurvey Project, where researchers return to the same locations he went to and examine how the flora and fauna have changed. He also published many influential papers, including one in which he coined the theory of the "ecological niche."

I feel just as honored to work with current scientists, such as my mentors, Theresa Barclay and Carla Cicero, and to help the lineage continue by teaching other students how to prepare birds. All of us are participating in one long-lived attempt to observe the world around us. We have come a long way, but there is still a long way to go. When I go out into the field, I see a kaleidoscope of organisms and interactions that we have only just barely started to understand. Within all of us lies the power to understand it—as long as we're willing to get a bit dirty.

TIPS

- If you are interested in learning how to prepare specimens, make sure you do so legally. Many birds in the United States are protected by the Migratory Bird Treaty Act. If you want to get involved, try finding taxidermy workshops or natural history museums near you.
- Invest in high-quality tools. You can find dissection scissors, scalpels, and forceps on Amazon.com and other online shopping sites.
- Even if you aren't interested in specimen preparation, visit a natural history museum near you. Everyone can learn something from hearing about the research conducted at museums, studying the history of the land, and seeing the variation between specimens.

IOANA SERITAN first picked up a pair of binoculars in 2010 and hasn't stopped talking about birds since. She is finishing her undergraduate studies at the University of California–Berkeley as a student of environmental sciences. She is an associate editor of the American Birding Association's *Birding* magazine. She can't pick one favorite bird, but among her favorites are rock pigeons, white-throated swifts, and Swainson's hawks.

The Meaning of Birds

by David A. La Puma

BIRDS ARE EVERYWHERE—IN EVERY WOODLOT, EVERY
city, every shopping mall, and every marsh. Birds are everywhere, and, with few exceptions, a bird can be found at all
times of year, anywhere you look. This is especially true for
someone like me who grew up in subtropical Florida and has
lived in either temperate or subtropical locales in the Northern Hemisphere throughout his life. I often can't help talking
endlessly about how birds are exceptional creatures, because
their diversity illustrates some of the most wonderful aspects
of biology: sexual selection, evolution, speciation, navigation,
and migration, for example. I am fascinated every day by
what new things I learn about and from birds. But ultimately,
their appeal is more primal, more basic. Birds are grounding.
Birds get me through.

Birds define periods of my life, and birding provides me
with an outlet for my emotions—a type of focused meditation. My father died in the spring. My memory of him
is inextricably tied to the arrival of early warblers, pine and

yellow-throated. The call of the blue-gray gnatcatcher, whiny as it may be, is also a reminder of how much my dad lamented tax day (I'm certain he died on that day out of spite). My mother died in late June, and immediately afterward I left home for Alaska, where my partner was doing fieldwork; we spent several weeks living out of a tent and exploring for birds I had seen only in field guides. We watched long-tailed jaegers on the tundra teaching their recently fledged young to hunt savannah sparrows, saw spectacled eiders on the Arctic Ocean, observed northern hawk-owl hunting from black spruce at the edge of the boreal forest, and heard the ethereal song of the varied thrush in the lush interior woods. A male pine grosbeak inquisitively peeked into our tent door, stunningly pink. My mother would have liked that bird.

On the morning of September 11, 2001, around 9 a.m., I walked into a Miami bank to cash a check. No tellers were present at the front desk when I entered, and I quickly realized that the three employees were crowded around a television set off in the corner of the office. The South Tower of the World Trade Center had been hit by a plane and was smoldering, and moments later a second plane struck the North Tower. What started as speculation about an accidental crash quickly turned to fear of something more sinister. Whether I ultimately cashed the check or just walked out, I can't remember. But when I think back on that day, I remember it in three periods: my morning birding prior to my trip to the bank, the time in the bank and the hours afterward watching the tragedy unfold on TV, while comforting friends who knew people who were killed in the World Trade Center attacks.

Only two hours prior to my trip to the bank I had been birding in a small park in a sea of concrete and steel—a perfect migrant-trap because it represented the only habitat for miles around. It wasn't a spectacular day in terms of bird diversity, but the birding had been good, and I'd seen a number of warblers, vireos, and one veery (causing that twitch of excitement for the day). Lucky for me, my notes are immortalized in online databases, so I can go back and see what I reported:

"I spent the morning at Barnes today checking for any new arrivals . . . what I found was low diversity but extreme abundance!'

It turns out that I had identified only nine species of warblers that day, but numbers of individuals were quite high. September 11 is early fall migration in Miami, and the species composition reflected it. Many northern parula, blue-gray gnatcatchers, and red-eyed vireos.

"Worm-eating warbler (not as many as two days ago, but still common): 30+."

That count really stands out to me, because since leaving Florida, any day when I see more than a few of these birds is quite notable.

Something else stands out, primarily because of its absence. My entry was time-stamped at 12:56 p.m., about two and a half hours after the second tower collapsed. I would have been in my girlfriend's dorm room at the time. In retrospect, I find this disconcerting. When I read back on my notes from that day, and the weeks that followed, I don't read the fear, the horror, or the pain associated with September 11, 2001. I know that I felt it, but I didn't document it, and I definitely didn't record it in my birding reports.

In more than a dozen years since the attacks, that tragic date has become synonymous with great birding, rather than new tragedies, and for this I am grateful to the birds (and also, somewhat, to humanity). My memories are of fallouts in Key West, big flights in Cape May, and even the annual turning on and off of the World Trade Center *Tribute* lights to allow nocturnally migrating songbirds to continue their migration without being entrained in the upward-facing beams.

Of course, as birds and life are inextricably linked, now, come September and October, my thoughts include the birth of our two daughters. Their birth dates are coincident with large diverse movements of warblers and heavy flights of raptors; the October songs of the Carolina wren; late-September nights with a telescope fixed on a full moon as small objects streak across it, *chip*s and *seep*s emanating from high above. Their season brings the sounds of migration, that fleeting period when birds embark on a ritual pilgrimage to escape the approaching winter, with its low food supply and extreme cold. Theirs is also the season of hope, of the knowledge that while migration is costly, it works; and soon enough the birds will return to produce young once more. I will be here. I will be waiting. I will welcome them.

TIPS

- *Follow the bird.* Migration was the hook that got me, and I ran with it, and I'd say that was the best thing I ever did. Find out what you love about birds and dive in; the pool of knowledge is deep and rich and full of others happy to help you along the way.
- *Bird locally, regionally, and globally.* Birding on your home turf repeatedly throughout the year will yield great insights into the rhythm of nature, help you better understand status and distribution of the birds that pass through your region, and allow you a lifetime of enjoyment with little investment in time and fossil fuels (all good!). But travel too. There is a wealth of knowledge to be gained by seeing and hearing species you are already familiar with in places you are not. You begin to see their whole range of experiences, habitats, and behaviors that come with these differences. Soon you will begin to really understand species when you see them throughout their life and geographic range. With over 10,000 species of bird on Earth, traveling to distant locales can be extremely rewarding and exciting. Birding festivals, organized trips by experienced tour outfits, and the

online birding community provide many opportunities to travel on a range of budgets and see many birds. Now get going!

- *Pay it forward.* Birds are an easy sell once you're hooked, but until hearing and seeing that bird was part of your "reality," it might as well have not existed at all. Help others tune in, turn on, and go birding! Pick up an extra copy of your favorite field guide and give it to someone you know who enjoys being outdoors. Take a neighbor birding in your local park, or even around your block. Do this with a bottle of wine or a pair of good beers along with the traditional binoculars and/or spotting scope.

▷▷•◁◁

DAVID LA PUMA is the director of New Jersey Audubon's Cape May Bird Observatory. His life's passion mirrors that of his organization's mission statement: to connect people to nature, and steward the nature of today for the people of tomorrow. When not working, David can be found walking the many birding haunts of Cape May, or pointing out birds to his daughters as they boogie-board together at their favorite beach.

Why I Love Being a Bird Photographer

by Marie Read

I'M ONE OF THOSE FANATICS WHO SPEND HOURS AT A TIME voluntarily imprisoned in a small canvas box, with one eye glued to the viewfinder of a camera, from the front of which protrudes a giant bazooka of a lens.

For me, there's nothing more engrossing than trying to capture the very essence of a bird with my camera. I lose myself entirely, waiting for the ideal lighting angle, the perfect turn of a head, the most dynamic pose, and, finally, the decisive moment when everything comes together and I create a frozen moment in time that reveals the bird's spirit.

My ultimate goal, of course, is to capture beautiful and exciting photographs, but being afield for long stretches of time, sometimes in the same spot, my actual experience is so much richer than the images I obtain. Thirty years of viewing life through a lens have given me a very special window into the avian world. I've lived vicariously through many events in birds' lives—most of them heartwarming, some even amusing, a few tragic and distressing, but all fascinating and engaging. Let me share some of my experiences with you.

A few years back, I photographed Baltimore orioles nesting high in a cottonwood tree. For fourteen days from hatch to fledge, I perched on a scaffolding tower each morning, swathed in camouflage, with my camera gear. Between bursts of activity when the adults fed the young, there were many times when not a darned thing was happening at that nest! Stuck as I was, in any other situation I might have been totally bored and restless during the downtimes. But it was Mother Nature's busiest season—all around me were the fascinating sights and sounds of birds' lives being lived full-tilt. And even though most were out of camera range, I had a ringside seat!

Early one morning, a flurry of activity caught my eye, and suddenly a miniature snippet of a life unfolded below me. In the raindrops gathered in the bowl of a large leaf, a female yellow warbler was taking a bath. Fluttering her tiny wings, she shimmied to and fro repeatedly, letting the water droplets thoroughly soak her plumage, and then began preening with such enthusiasm as to make the leaf wobble wildly. Finally, satisfactorily spruced up, she gave a final shake—wings whirring and water drops flying—before setting off on her busy quest for breakfast. Total time for the warbler's morning ritual? About three and a half minutes. But for me, it was as if time had stopped completely, so enthralled was I with the tiny bird's behavior.

To enjoy watching birds, nothing beats acting like you're part of the scenery. Concealing yourself in a blind is great: birds usually don't realize you're there. In addition to lens ports, most good photo blinds have small mesh-covered viewing windows through which you can carefully peer, although your view of the surroundings will be limited. Even without a blind, if you wear quiet-colored clothing and sit still and quiet, birds will eventually ignore you and go about their normal lives. And all your senses will come into play—sound, vision, even smell.

In a stinky Panamanian swamp, I was once treated to the ear-splitting cacophonous duet of a pair of gray-necked wood-rails walking no more than a yard away from my blind. Closer to home, a belted kingfisher once landed on top of my blind. Just inches above my head I could see her little feet shadowed through the fabric and hear her soft, rattled calls, a much-muted version of the shrill sound we usually associate with this species. Another time, a green heron entertained me by crazily running to and fro along the edge of a pond, ducking and weaving while being dive-bombed by a swarm of irritated barn swallows that had been gathering mud for their nests.

Occasionally, I've been deeply shaken by the rawness of nature. While I sat rock-still with my camera on the shore of California's Mono Lake, hundreds of Wilson's phalaropes began landing nearby, and in the space of an hour they had settled to rest all around me. Suddenly the peaceful scene was shattered when a peregrine falcon rocketed in and, in the blink of an eye, seized a phalarope in its talons right before my eyes, sending the remaining flock into an explosion of panic.

You needn't be a photographer to have such experiences. But you *do* need to allow yourself time to watch birds closely. Sit quietly in a comfortable spot, breathe deeply, and let nature happen all around you.

For a bird photographer, time spent simply watching pays dividends. The knowledge you'll gain about bird behavior will improve your photography immensely. You'll notice the subtle behavior cues birds give before doing something cool and dramatic—a duck performing its courtship display, an eagle taking flight, or a waxwing tossing back a berry. Once you recognize these signals, you can anticipate those photogenic activities in the future and, who knows, maybe you'll capture a prize-winning shot. Furthermore, when you're in one location for long periods of time, other photo opportunities may reveal themselves.

Getting back to that oriole nest, I had the bittersweet thrill of witnessing the baby orioles fledging. Over the days, their begging became ever louder and they became more adventurous, first taking tentative peeks at the world, and soon growing strong enough to sit on the rim of the nest and exercise their wings. On the final morning, one after another the four youngsters clambered out of the nest. With fluttering wings they made their way up into the tree to join their waiting parents, thus beginning a new stage of their lives. For me—left gazing at an empty nest—it was a heart-tuggingly poignant moment.

At its best, bird photography is exciting and rewarding, but it's also challenging, time-consuming, and sometimes just plain frustrating. But being behind that camera is what motivates me to be outside and keeps me out there enjoying the wonderful world of birds for far longer than I would otherwise. And that's always good for the soul.

TIPS
- Take your time, breathe deeply. Think of bird watching as meditation—a way of being good to yourself. As you become calmer, your senses will open to the bird activities around you.
- Pick a comfortable place to sit, where you can keep low, still, and quiet. Try a folding stool (such as Walkstool®) or a fold-up seat (such as Crazy Creek Chair®). Wear muted-color clothing or camouflage.
- For photographers, it helps to have your camera and lens on a tripod. That way, when you want to take a shot you will not have to raise the camera and possibly spook your bird. Using a tripod eliminates having to hold your camera in position while you wait for the decisive moment;

holding it in your hands for long periods of time gets tiring, and you may miss the shot.

BIRD PHOTOGRAPHER MARIE READ's images appear regularly in nature magazines, books, and calendars worldwide. Her distinctive photographic style highlights birds' fascinating life histories as well as their lively beauty. She has authored many magazine articles about birds, bird behavior, and bird photography, as well as several books, including *Secret Lives of Common Birds* and *Into the Nest* (the latter coauthored with Laura Erickson).

Why I Love Birding in Mexico

by Steve N. G. Howell

MEXICO IS A MAGICAL LAND, FULL OF AMAZING BIRDS, not to mention culture and cuisine. Yes, "things" can happen, as in any country, including my native Britain, but these simply add to the experience of travel and often have a comic aspect when one is familiar with the country and culture. So what's it really like birding south of the border?

There are a few reasons you might be scared about going to Mexico. It's clear from reading and watching the media that you'd be lucky to even get out of the airport without being shot by some drug traffickers, and if you do make it out of the airport, then, well, who knows what might happen? You might spend the morning watching a tree full of feeding Aztec thrushes and brown-backed solitaires, while a handsome male cinnamon-bellied flowerpiercer flits around in the flowers below, feisty Mexican violetears sing from every side, a roaming flock of garrulous gray-barred wrens brings with them the incredible chestnut-sided shrike-vireo, and a migrant olive-sided flycatcher watches over it all from atop a towering fir tree. In fact, this all happened to me just this morning, and I'm still alive.

While I was absorbing this "just another amazing hour in Mexico," the rest of the world ceased to exist. Wars, stock markets, politics—all forgotten. I think this is a big part of watching birds for many people: in the moment, the only things that exist are you and the bird. Birding is a priceless commodity. But why Mexico? Let me think about that as I head out for an open-air, fresh seafood dinner overlooking the beach, a warm breeze wafting in off the Pacific . . .

It's inevitable that in my thirty years of leading tours in Mexico some things have happened, and here I'll mention just a few from one of my favorite birding areas, Colima, where we see over three hundred bird species in a week of great birding in warm sunny weather, with a smoking volcano as a backdrop. Fortunately, nothing very serious has ever transpired—well, okay, that vagrant black thrush years ago on the volcanoes was pretty serious, and exciting. Perhaps the worst thing was once locking the keys in the van, way up on the volcanoes. Fortunately, one window was open a little, and a long branch enabled me to unhook the keys from the ignition and delicately, oh so delicately, pull them out.

Then there was the time when a guy nearly punched me in the *zócalo*. (No, that's not a euphemism for a tender body part—it's the Mexican word for plaza, which is the center of evening life in every Mexican town.) It was Valentine's Day, and on each table the restaurant had tied red-heart balloons around the ends of drinking straws. My coleader decided we should take the balloons and drive around the *zócalo* after dinner with the group, and hand out the hearts to the prettiest girls we saw. Imagine a girl's surprise when a van full of gringos stops, a crazy-looking bearded guy she's never seen before gets out, runs over, and presents her with a Valentine heart! And her boyfriend? He was stunned long enough for me to smile and dash back to the van as he was pulling back his arm! Yes, Mexico could be dangerous!

On one trip, our trusty restaurant of many years was closed down and I needed a new venue, not so easy to find in a small rural town. I found a place that normally closed at 6 p.m., but they agreed to stay open just for our group (birders often don't keep "normal" hours). They made some amazing *carne asada* tacos, great beans, and salad, served with cold beer, and we ate there the next night as well. By then we were all friends and the owner presented me with a shot glass, which he proceeded to fill and insist I take with me as a parting gift (yes, I still have it). Fortunately, walking down the street and sipping tequila is not a problem in Mexico, where common sense still reigns over rigidly applied rules for the sake of rules.

And that time the guys with automatic weapons jumped from the back of a pickup and pulled us over was "just another day in Mexico." We were on a new stretch of toll highway with basically no traffic when the truck up ahead turned ninety degrees, blocking all lanes, and said guys with said guns leaped out. I think my group was a little surprised, alarmed even, but I pulled over, greeted the seeming *banditos* with *"Buenas tardes,"* and asked what they wanted. They were just *federales* on a training exercise, very polite, and a little embarrassed that they'd picked a gringo van. I told them we didn't have any arms or drugs on board, but that the next van coming along might be a different story. We drove off waving and looked in the mirror to see the *federales* pull over the next van, containing my coleader with his half of the group. He was also Mexico-savvy, however, and we all had a good laugh about it.

I had to dredge my memory for these "bad" stories, but not so for bird images, which spring unbidden: a million male yellow-headed blackbirds swirling in swarms that blackened the skies; an eared poorwill singing point-blank in the spotlight; the little-known white-fronted swift circling low over a quiet beach road; my first ever thick-billed parrots (a flock of sixty, raucously laughing as they sailed overhead in the morning sun); two vagrant red-throated pipits at the airport marshes; and on and on. But one of the best things about birding in Mexico is sharing it with others and seeing their reactions to the wonderful birds, scenery, food, and, of course, the friendly people—which reminds me of one last story.

We were looking for banded quail on a quiet side road when two men called to us from a gateway. One was over six feet tall, the proverbial brick outhouse, with a tattooed shaved head, and I could sense some of the group flinch—he looked like a gang member from Los Angeles. After the traditional *"Buenas tardes"* greetings, he asked what we were doing. When we answered, he had some questions, the first of which was "What's the beautiful little blue bird we see around here?" It was an orange-breasted bunting, and when he learned they occurred only in Mexico I could sense a little pride. As it turned out, he spoke English (having worked somewhere in California), which meant the group could understand what he said. He lived on the ranch here, with his brother, and was so much happier back home than in the crazy world of California. Moreover, he invited us through the gate and pointed to a field where he said we could see quail—and we did!

TIPS

- Always be willing to travel to foreign countries.
- Treat the people you meet as you'd like to be treated.
- Learn a little Spanish—it really helps.

STEVE N. G. HOWELL is an international bird tour leader with WINGS, a research associate at the California Academy of Sciences, and a popular speaker and trip leader at birding festivals. He has authored numerous books and articles, mainly about birds, including the *Peterson Reference Guide to Molt in North American Birds*. The common thread through Steve's life is that birding should be fun.

Color y Calor

by Catherine Hamilton

I SIT ON THE DECK OF OUR LODGE, WATCHING AN astonishing array of tropical birds as they come into the feeders here. It is siesta hour. We are north of Boca Tapada, Costa Rica, and somewhere just south of the Nicaraguan border, and it is hot and humid in a way that makes my mind attempt to get out of my body. I drink a Coke, sans ice, and curl my bare feet back from the line on the wood floor where the afternoon sun is advancing. As is usual for this kind of trip, I have been up since before 5 a.m., slapping at flies and sweating the entire time. The three of us have already spent eight hours birding the lowland rainforest here, and have a probable four or so more before calling it a day. This is a serious birding venture: there are species to be confirmed for range maps, fragmented habitats to be verified and categorized.

My drink is at least cool, and sans ice only because there is none to be had, not because I distrust the water. I am not worried about the water here. I am wary of the sun, though, and am sitting as close to the edge of the open deck as possible without leaving its shade. I want to be as near to the bananas as I can. There is a banana bunch hanging from a tree in front of me. The bananas host a stream of brightly colored birds. What I am trying to say is that I want to paint the birds. There are brown-hooded parrots, keel-billed and chestnut-mandibled toucans, red-legged and green honeycreepers, Passerini's tanagers, and Montezuma oropendolas—living palettes whose hues shift drastically as they move in and out of the sunlight, at one moment blinding, then the next glowing eerily from the shadows.

We are on this trip to locate rarer birds than the ones that frequent lodge feeders, but if these are the commoners, I am not complaining. The fluctuation of color temperature on these birds is enough to melt my mind. I look at them, and then at my watercolor palette, where rivers of brilliant and pure color run together to discover conflict. The chaos of overly mixed watercolor is not pretty, and the humidity is not helping, as nothing is drying, and I am sluggish. In this crazy tropical environment, my palette tends to end up a swirly, muddy mess, and if ever there were a reason to use garish color, straight out of the tube, these birds are it. I open another tepid Coke.

Cola-fueled electrons modestly bouncing, my thoughts wander. The sun has advanced. I move myself back another few inches, and see that my feet have left damp footprints behind on the wood. I am now gawking at two golden-hooded tanagers, and am sketching a keel-billed toucan: have you ever really looked at the array of hues on that magnificent bill? Where someone might see just a beak, I am looking at a riot of colors, and shapes made by those colors, and at the light reflected off of the environs. I am ostensibly drawing a bird, its parts, its body, but when I get to the edge of a bird perhaps I also want to look at the plants around it, or its larger habitat, or its habitat over the course of a full year, or the habitats at the edge of its habitats . . . How does one define the boundaries? Do I decide that colors end at the edge of a bird, or do I extend them outward, affected by air or environment, light reflected off of the green of a bromeliad, the highlights of a tropical sun? Where does a bird end and its habitat begin? How do you get those concepts into a drawing?

Field sketching is amazing, something to spend a life learning from. It teaches you to see things deeply, teaches more about proportion and structure and field marks than less involved methods of looking. It unquestionably improves one's birding skill, artist or no; it doesn't even really matter, in this context, what the drawing looks like, because the lessons are learned during the act of seeing. But it doesn't just improve one's understanding of a bird as a species and how to recognize that species. It also gives you a way of looking at the world beyond it. That color on a bird's belly is not just one color from a field guide; there are also the colors of light that have passed through and bounced off of its surroundings.

At a certain point, the observation of a bird—its color or field marks, or its posture or pose—encompasses not only what that bird is or what it is doing, but also what that bird *might* do. Then, while out birding, there is intuition, or perhaps imagination, and there is the tingle of anticipation you get when you realize that a particular species could be here, right here, right now. This is a synthesis of looking and learning, and being aware that there is a larger system than drawing an outline around one species and being able to differentiate it from another. It is this synthesis, a layering of new mysteries and questions over experience, that draws me out into the field, over and over again.

TIPS

I am addicted to this life of birding, and looking, and questioning, and drawing, always drawing. As an artist, it is the backbone of my entire being, but for anyone, it can be a remarkably worthwhile (and fun!) endeavor. I have five bits of advice for the reader who is already thinking, "Oh, I can't do that!"

1. You can.
2. Never think of the drawing you are working on as your ultimate work. The goal is for your twentieth sketch to be better than your first, not to make a perfect drawing on the first go.

3. Look at the birds more than you look at your paper. You will have to trust me on this. See tip 2.

4. Birds move. This is frustrating. If you spend some time following tip 3, however, you will start to see that they also resume similar positions, act out similar behaviors. Your drawing of one bird could comprise multiple birds, or multiple sightings of the same bird. For a respite, find larger birds that aren't moving as much.

5. Take a class, or join a field sketching or nature journaling group. These are generally very supportive, and within one class or workshop you can learn a lot from the other participants, from absolute beginners to seasoned pros. This makes for unique opportunities and inspirations. Whether your goal is to make coherent birding field notes and sketches or to make artistic masterpieces, this will guarantee to improve your seeing and skills.

CATHERINE HAMILTON was pretty much born with a pencil in hand, and began birding at an early age with her father. A professional exhibiting artist for over twenty-five years, she has recently been sharing her passion through speaking, teaching, and guiding tours. Catherine loves working with birders and artists of all levels, and believes that anyone can gain a greater understanding of the world around them through field sketching and observation.

el sueño
de las aves
produce
¡aves!

Class Outside

by Jonathan Rosen

WHEN I BEGAN BIRD WATCHING IN MY EARLY THIRTIES, I often found myself wishing, on my first forays, that I had started as a child. How wonderful if I had absorbed all those names, shapes, sounds, and patterns back when I had infinite memory and time, like a child learning a language in the cradle. Birds would be my mother tongue—or at least a fluent second language. Instead, there I was, flipping frantically through the Peterson Field Guide like a tourist hunting through a Berlitz phrase book; by the time I blurted out the word "redstart," the beautiful stranger was gone.

Now that I am in my early fifties, of course, I am grateful that I began when I did. Perhaps if I had taken up karate I'd be a triple black belt. Perhaps. But even though I am only a yellow-belted birder at best, I understand that from the beginning something radically new and unexpected began happening to me. It went beyond the excitement of seeing beautiful wild animals passing through my city, and beyond the thrill of stalking, finding, and identifying them.

Certainly I felt my capacity for wonder renewed and my isolated human self reconnecting to the larger web of the natural world and its seasons. But I am talking about something different. I may have failed in my earliest efforts to look up birds that did not perch with the patience of nineteenth-century statesmen posing for daguerreotypes, but soon enough my mind was thrumming with words and pictures. A raft of names as new and beautiful as the birds themselves—blue-winged teal, prothonotary warbler, indigo bunting—or as awkward as the people who watch them—yellow-rumped warbler, rufous-sided towhee, great crested flycatcher—had taken up permanent residence in my brain. They flew out of my mouth almost before I knew I was saying them.

I am tempted to say that my brain felt younger, but I have to admit that when I was young my brain was a constant geriatric disappointment. The sports statistics that my friends devoured and spat out like watermelon seeds I swallowed and never saw again. The multiplication tables, the names of state capitals, the spelling of almost any word loaded onto mental shelves in my early plastic years are not there now—in part because they were never really there then.

But from the moment I began going outside with binoculars and a field guide, alone or with a group, I was aware that the furniture of my mind was rearranging itself. My brain made room for birds and for all that they brought with them: Latin names and common names; bird song, range maps, breeding plumage. My appetite for information and my ability to remember it—my capacity *for learning itself*—seemed to have doubled. My brain had gotten not younger but wiser.

Why? What had happened and how had it happened? I have always loved words; I was an English major in college and I make my living as a writer. The physical act of reading, however, and by extension the kind of learning that relies on decoding and retrieval, was always labor.

It took me many years to answer what at the time did not even feel like a question, more like an awakened ability that I associated with being outdoors and superstitiously let be. It took my daughters being born and going to school in a more enlightened age than my own in order for me to understand what bird watching had unlocked. It was my daughters' struggles with reading, and their conquest of those struggles, that finally taught me what was going on.

Both my daughters are dyslexic. My wife, who is not, was plowing through a quaint and curious volume of language-based learning disability lore one day when she looked up and said to me, "This is you." And so it was.

It turns out that the educational methods best suited to overcoming dyslexia are almost all an organic part of bird watching. For people with dyslexia, learning is facilitated by a multisensory approach that lets you see and hear and even touch words in an environment that engages the whole self. Repetition is also enormously important, but so is avoiding the boredom that comes with repetition. I did not get bored taking out a guide book on the subway and looking through the warblers between stops—magnolia, Cape May, Wilson's—with the added incentive of wondering if I might be lucky enough to see a real live one in the woods. I did not get bored jotting down the names of the birds I saw, reading them again at home as I checked them off, and maybe looking them up again—possibly in more than one book—to confirm that's what I'd really seen.

Flipping through a guidebook turned out to be only a small part of getting to know the birds. I looked through field guides at home, associating bird names with bird pictures; I looked through guidebooks in the woods, associating bird names and bird pictures with living birds moving through the air or perched in a tree. There was seeing and hearing the birds, and the birds seeing and hearing me—or at least reacting to my presence if I was close, so that my whole body was on alert.

There was listening to bird song at home on CD (in the early days) or with an MP3 player as time passed. There was learning the mnemonic devices that are built into bird song—*sweet sweet I'm so sweet* for the yellow warbler; *pleased pleased pleased to MEETCHA* for the chestnut-sided warbler. There was listening to the song, seeing the picture, and reading the name at home. There was listening to real birds sing outside.

There was seeing the bird and hearing the bird, saying the name of the bird aloud, and hearing other people say the name aloud. There was turning from the book to the bird, and from the bird back to the book, until the world of words and the world of unarticulated life were doing a kind of endless dance.

Imagine a history book that did half of that. There goes a black-capped Napoleon chased by a one-armed Nelson! Is that the Marseillaise? No, it's the Napoleon, singing: *He who fears being conquered is sure of defeat.*

In fact, books can do that more and more. My daughters get digitized textbooks on their computers, which read aloud to them while they follow the words on the screen. While this is a special accommodation, clearly there is something satisfying about combining the eyes and the ears because Amazon now offers books to the general public that pair the audio and digital so that you can read and listen together. You can make notes in one platform that show up in another. My field guides are now all on my phone, putting pictures and sounds and words in one interactive place.

Technology has always been a part of bird watching—paradoxically, perhaps, because bird watching feels so natural, but we are paradoxical creatures. We interpose binoculars, those manmade miracles, between birds and ourselves, and yet they bring us closer to nature rather than distancing us from it. The birds are paradoxical, too—creatures of earth and sky. Our learning works best when it is grounded in the body, even if it enables mental flight.

In one of his most famous letters, the great romantic poet John Keats explained his theory of life to his brother and sister-in-law. The world, he wrote, was a school "instituted for the purpose of teaching little children to read." For Keats, reading means much more than decoding words, and the end result is much more than the acquisition of knowledge. The child, using the heart and the mind, interprets the world, a human activity that paradoxically generates the immortal part of the self, which Keats calls the soul. He calls the world "the vale of soul making."

I love Keats's notion of soul making even though it sometimes eludes me. What I like best about it is the idea that the world is a school, but an unconventional one. It has trees, for example, and grass. It requires the whole self to learn. And it is the kind of place where, if you are lucky, you might find children and animals who will teach you the secrets of life.

TIPS
- *Dyslexia* is the name we give a cluster of symptoms that, in their aggregate, constitute a language-based learning disability. However variable, the disorder is not hard to diagnose and remediate. A great place to start is the In-

ternational Dyslexia Association website: https://dyslexia
ida.org.

- Birds don't care about ornithology, but it is helpful for humans to have names and categories for experience, especially if the experience is making a child feel frustrated. The board of education will test your child and suggest appropriate accommodations if any are needed.

- A lot of children—and adults—have no trouble reading books but cannot read the natural world at all. I urge everyone to get kids outside and looking up. I'm a fan of *The Young Birder's Guide to Birds of North America* by Bill Thompson III, but I think birding apps are a great way to bring sound, sight, and language together. And *What the Robin Knows: How Birds Reveal the Secrets of the Natural World* by Jon Young is full of ways of watching that parents can pass on to children.

- *My Dyslexia* is a wonderful book by the poet Philip Schultz, who discovered his dyslexia in middle age, or rather, the name for what had previously been a private torment. He also discovered that he isn't a poet *in spite of* his disability but because of it. So don't forget that dyslexia which has nothing to do with intelligence, is really a *difference* as much as a *disability*—just not if it's ignored.

>▷•◁<

JONATHAN ROSEN is the author of two novels, *Eve's Apple* and *Joy Comes in the Morning,* and two works of nonfiction, *The Talmud and the Internet: A Journey Between Worlds* and *The Life of the Skies: Birding at the End of Nature.* His essays and articles have appeared in *The New Yorker,* the *New York Times Magazine,* the *Atlantic, Audubon,* and numerous anthologies. He is working on a book about friendship and mental illness for Penguin Press.

Why I Love the Way Birding Helps Us Learn

by Jennie Duberstein

IN THE SPRING OF 1998, I WAS ON A BOAT IN THE MIDDLE OF Lake Pátzcuaro in the western Mexico state of Michoacán. I was working as the youth program coordinator for Colorado Bird Observatory (now Bird Conservancy of the Rockies). My boss had brought me along on a teacher exchange that was part of our program that linked classrooms in Colorado with classrooms in western Mexico through migratory birds. At the time, I spoke almost no Spanish, but I welcomed the opportunity to visit a new country, meet new people, and see new birds.

My lack of Spanish got in the way of conversation almost immediately. I got by with my small stockpile of nouns, a few poorly conjugated verbs, and many wild gestures. But that day on the boat, as I stood next to one of the biologists, we realized that although I didn't really speak Spanish and he didn't really speak English, we could talk to each other in our common language of the Latin names of the birds we were seeing. *"Dendroica petechia,"* he said, gesturing at a nearby yellow warbler. I suddenly wished I'd spent more time memorizing the Latin names of birds in my college ornithology class. I have to admit, I remember almost none of the birds I saw that day off the top of my head, but I have a very clear memory of us talking about yellow warblers and describing in English and Spanish how they sound. (Incidentally, *"sweet sweet sweet I'm so sweet"* doesn't quite translate into Spanish.)

Birding helped us transcend the language barrier. It also motivated me to really buckle down and learn Spanish, as well as scientific names.

Fast-forward almost twenty years. Recently I was helping lead a youth field trip in Tucson. This was a group of high school students with no prior birding experience. The kids were refugees—their families had settled in Tucson after fleeing their homes in different African countries: Somalia, Rwanda, Uganda, Democratic Republic of Congo, and elsewhere. Some of them had been in the United States for only a few months. Some spoke almost no English. I can only begin to imagine what kinds of things these kids and their families experienced before they ended up in Tucson. They were part of a special program to help them connect with and explore the natural world in their new home.

We had a few ground rules. Since English was the only language we all had in common, we would all speak English (unless someone was helping to translate for someone who just couldn't understand). And we left our cell phones at the field station.

I knew ahead of time that the diversity of English levels would make the use of a standard field guide difficult, so I put together a mini field guide of six common birds, with a few bullets for each describing the bird, how it behaved, and its diet.

We split up the kids into teams, each with an assigned bird. I quickly realized that even my simple field guides were too complex for this group. Diet? What does that mean? A curved bill? What's a bill?

After about five seconds of feeling flustered because my lesson couldn't go according to plan, I soon realized that birds were about to transcend boundaries again. *Well, let's use birds to teach English,* I thought. I explained the word *diet.* My group's bird was the Anna's hummingbird. We talked about insects and nectar and other things that hummingbirds and other birds might eat. "What is *your* diet?" I asked one of the young women in my group. She quickly caught on and described her favorite Somali dish. The vocabulary lesson continued as I described the diet of a house finch, a vermilion flycatcher, a red-tailed hawk: seed, insect, mammal. As a complete bonus, by the end of the day I had also learned a few words in Somali, Arabic, and Swahili.

It wasn't just about the kids learning new words and practicing English. It helped me think of new ways to describe

things that were so familiar to me that I'd almost forgotten how to describe them. Birding teaches us new vocabulary and helps us practice our common language(s).

We hopped on the streetcar and rode over to the University of Arizona campus (birding helped introduce us to ways to get around a new city). This was the perfect spot for beginning birders: not a ton of diversity, but really great looks at a few species.

One young man was very reserved. Based on his body language, it didn't seem like he was having much fun. I'd been given a heads-up by the other leader that he was often like this, but that he kept coming back week after week to their field trips, so he clearly wanted to be there. As we stopped to look at an Anna's hummingbird perched at the top of a mesquite tree, I noticed he was looking at a different spot than the rest of the group. I tried to direct him to the bird, but he knew what he was doing—he'd discovered some mourning doves perched in a different part of the tree. He helped me get them into the spotting scope to share with the rest of the group. As I quietly complimented him on his excellent observation skills, I could see him respond, and he was more engaged for the rest of the field trip. He found more and different birds than any other participant on the trip and excitedly shared them with the rest of the group. Birding is a common experience that helps us feel comfortable and gives us opportunities to both learn and teach, no matter who we are.

We walked about a quarter mile, birding along the way, until we got to a small garden. A broad-billed hummingbird made an appearance. A vermilion flycatcher was sallying out from his perch, hunting insects. Verdins were calling all over the place. I spotted one verdin nest, and a young woman joyfully spotted about six more in nearby trees. Everyone practiced whistling verdin calls. Birding helps us learn to be observant.

I had the students sit down with their field journals and colored pencils. The instruction: draw something that you saw today. After all the kids were done with their drawings, we shared the sketches with each other and talked a bit about other information that might be good to include with their drawings. Everyone added the date and location. Birding helps us practice writing in a new language.

After a rousing game of ultimate Frisbee (birding: sometimes you need a break, especially when you are just starting out), we hopped back on the streetcar. We had to walk a few blocks from the streetcar stop back to the field station, but it took us at least twenty minutes because the kids kept stopping to look at birds. One of the final birds of the day was a Cooper's hawk that buzzed our heads to a chorus of astonished gasps and exclamations (birding helps us notice and appreciate the extraordinary in everyday life).

The last thing we did was enter our eBird checklist (birding helps us learn new technology). It was remarkable the way the kids remembered every species that we saw. If they couldn't remember the name of the bird, they described what it looked like or pulled up the picture in the field guide. We saw a total of ten species that day, and I couldn't have been more excited if we'd seen 110.

That day was a good reminder that birding isn't always about the birds we see (or even the ones we miss). There are so many things that we can learn from birding, from the obvious (skills that help us identify and appreciate birds in the field) to the less so—for instance, I have learned an awful lot about myself and human nature as a result of the time I have spent outside looking for birds.

TIPS

- "If you're not making mistakes, you're not trying hard enough." I heard Michael O'Brien say this, years ago, to a group of young birders. His advice transcends birding. Don't be afraid to make mistakes or to admit when you have. It is okay to be wrong. We all are, a lot of the time. Mistakes are how we learn.

- Everyone has something to teach others, whether you mentor a young birder, lead a walk at your local nature center, or make changes in your everyday life in ways that support bird conservation.

- There is always more to learn, often in unexpected places, and from unexpected people.

Jennie Duberstein coordinates the Sonoran Joint Venture, a binational partnership to conserve the unique birds and habitats of the southwestern United States and northwestern Mexico. She studies the human dimensions of conservation, working with people to find solutions to the complex issues facing our natural world. Jennie has worked with young birders since the late 1990s, directing summer camps, organizing conferences, and managing and editing young-birder publications.

Bird Songs, Birders,
and Musicians

by Bill Thompson III

I GREW UP IN A HOUSE FULL OF MUSIC. MY DAD WAS A JAZZ piano player and my mom a singer—in fact, they met when Mom auditioned for Dad's jazz combo in college— so it seemed natural to me that the air around our family was always full of music. When I became a bird watcher at a very young age, I felt drawn to bird songs. I can vividly recall the first time I heard a male northern cardinal singing in my Grandma Thompson's backyard on a hot summer after- noon. Later, when my birding became more focused, I found that identifying birds by their songs came easily to me. It's not that I spent any meaningful time studying recordings of bird songs—I didn't. And it's not that I took years of music lessons—didn't do that either. My love of human-made music and bird song, I believe, came from growing up surrounded by music. My ears were already attuned to hearing the music of the birds.

There is a deep emotional connection that most humans

have with music. We can be moved to tears of joy or sorrow from a simple passage in a song. Many of our most memorable moments have a song or other music associated with them. I suppose that is why we add music to our birthdays, our holidays, our marriages, and funerals. We humans love a soundtrack behind our activities.

I have spent most of my adult life doing two things: birding and playing music. I've done both on a professional level for decades, though I'll never earn a Ph.D. in ornithology, nor will I ever perform in Carnegie Hall. Still, I love to ponder the music-and-birds connection, if only from my own rich experience and on an anecdotal, rather than scientific, basis.

We are taught not to anthropomorphize (ascribing human characteristics to birds), but it's hard to dismiss the fervent singing of a male prairie warbler (or any songbird, for that matter) delivered at the height of spring courtship from the best perch in his territory. In that moment, this tiny, feathered Pavarotti is expressing his fiery desire to mate, to make more prairie warblers that are just like him: beautiful, musical, and skillful enough to hold down a prime territory. Is it just the drive to procreate and pass on a genetic lineage that moves the male prairie warbler to sing at dawn each spring morning? Or do birds have souls and feelings? And, if so, do they find these songs to be deeply pleasing to sing and hear? Can we ever know this?

What we do know is that some of the music that many

birds make is learned while in the nest, or even still inside the egg, and some is apparently preprogrammed into a chick's DNA. Ornithologists have discovered that in some songbirds, the preprogrammed material is a rudimentary version of the fully formed song, usually sung by adult males of that species but recognized by males and females. The more detailed aspects of an individual bird's song are added later, when the hatchling is in the nest, hearing its male parent singing nearby. Some evidence exists that this learning may actually occur before hatching, when the fully formed, about-to-hatch bird hears the song through the walls of the shell. Birds such as warblers, finches, buntings, vireos, wrens, and others with complex songs acquire their "music" in this way. And that's the same way I acquired mine—by hearing my parents' music all around our home "nest" before I fledged.

Let's go back to the affinity between musicians and birders. Most humans with any degree of music aptitude recognize scales: a series of notes, going up or down in pitch, at whole or half changes in tone. Scales come in modes, defined by their patterns: major, minor, and a bunch of other names like Dorian, Lydian, and Mixolydian. Birds do not sing precisely in any of our known modes or scales, though some, like the musician wrens of South America, come very close. Yet their music is pleasing to our ears, and we can hear a bird song and know which species is singing it. How cool is that?

Among my birding friends, the best by-ear birders are the

musicians or music lovers, several of whom have essays in this book. Why are so many birders musicians, and vice versa? I believe there are several possible reasons.

A person with a sensitive ear-to-brain connection can hear things that others may not. I have many musician friends who have what's known as *perfect pitch*. In other words, you can play a note on any instrument, and they can tell you what note it is. These people, apparently, have some kind of internal pitchfork that registers a single, fixed tone. They use this tone to recognize other tones and identify them based on the interval between them. If I play an E for my friend Josh, he knows that it's two whole tones above middle C and can immediately identify it. My friend Wendy can pick out a single off-key note in a chorus of voices or the single string that's off-pitch in a twelve-string guitar. My music buddy John can hear a song once, then pick up his guitar and play it almost perfectly. Ability like this, which is a miracle to me, comes naturally to them. All three of these people are master musicians and all three have at least a passing interest in birds. When I've taken each of them birding, they quickly pick up on birding by ear—much more quickly than the average person might. I suspect these same folks, and others like them, would learn a new language with great facility, too. After all, music is language for birds, as well as for humans.

And yet I've heard beginning and intermediate birders say to me hundreds if not thousands of times over the years: "I just don't get bird songs. They all sound the same to me. Birding by ear is so frustrating!"

I recall that feeling as a new birder. A May morning sounded like a dozen orchestras and marching bands all playing at the same time. But then I absorbed the songs of a few common resident birds, and slowly the songs fell into place. A technique that helped me learn was to hear an unfamiliar song and follow it until I found the singer. One spring, after years of following songs to the singers, things finally clicked, and spring bird songs made sense to me. I could hear the subtle differences in pattern, tone, pitch, and rhythm, in much the same way most of us can tell the Beatles from the Rolling Stones, Count Basie from Glenn Miller, and Bach from Beethoven.

Some of my most wonderful, memorable birding moments are associated with bird song—like that male northern cardinal singing *what-cheer-cheer-cheer-cheer* from the magnolia tree in my grandma's backyard. I can still see him, surrounded by shiny, deep-green leaves, against the cloudless blue summer sky. The first time I heard a veery's cascading flute song, I got chills down my spine because it was so hauntingly beautiful. And the unmusical *peent* of a male American woodcock, heard each March in our hay meadow, reassures me that spring is coming.

If you are a musician, or simply enjoy listening to music, try tuning your musical ear to the songs and sounds of birds.

It may or may not help you improve your birding-by-ear skills, but it will surely add a beautiful dimension to your connection with the natural world. The birds are out there, right now, singing. We should take every opportunity to be out there with them, listening.

TIPS

- *Follow the song.* One of the best ways to learn a bird's song or call is to go find out who is singing. When you hear an unfamiliar song or call, follow it until you can see the bird that's making the sound. This can be very helpful in remembering the association between song and singer by anchoring the audible with the visual.

- *Compare to the familiar.* When you hear an unfamiliar song, try to compare it to the song of a species that you know well. Is the mystery song hoarser than a robin's song? Is it more complicated than a yellow warbler's song? Is it thinner-sounding than a song sparrow's song? Use familiar songs to help you determine how a song is different, which can often lead to a positive identification.

- *Use mnemonics.* Barred owls don't really call out *Who cooks for YOU? Who cooks for YOU all?* but the cadence of their typical nine-hoot call *sounds* like that's what they're saying. Same thing with the *Chi-CAH-go!* call of the Gambel's quail. These are bird-song *mnemonics* (knee-

MON-ics)—a word- or sound-based memory device that helps you associate a short phrase with a bird's song or call. Field guides are full of them, but you can also come up with your own mnemonics to help you remember bird sounds.

B ILL THOMPSON III is the editor and publisher of *Bird Watcher's Digest,* the bimonthly birding magazine launched in 1978. The author of many books on birds and nature, including *The New Birder's Guide to Birds of North America,* Bill also hosts *This Birding Life,* a podcast for birders that enjoys a worldwide audience. He is founder of the American Birding Expo and a popular speaker and guide at birding festivals. He is the leader and guitar player/singer for the country-rock band the Rain Crows, which plays all original music.

Watching Birds Watch Birds

by Sheri L. Williamson

IT WAS A COOL BUT SUNNY MORNING DURING FALL migration, and the yard was bustling with bird activity. Hordes of ravenous lesser goldfinches swarmed the nyjer sock, a flock of Gambel's quail crowded three deep at the water feature, a handful of newly arrived white-crowned sparrows scrounged seeds dropped by the resident pyrrhuloxias, and five descendants of red jungle fowl—our pet hens Joni, Grace, Layla, Dixie, and Lucy—chased grasshoppers, scratched in the dirt, and basked in the autumn sun.

From a chair on the patio, I scanned the action while sipping from a mug of bird-friendly (shade-grown organic) coffee. Our flightier feeder visitors would normally shy away from my intimidating size and predator-like forward-facing eyes, but the chickens' relaxed demeanor put them at ease with the message: *We trust the featherless biped*. As long as I didn't make any sudden moves (flexing a creaky joint, flipping the page of a magazine, or sipping from the aforementioned mug), they'd go about their routine as if I weren't there.

With their minds off me, the wild birds could concentrate on more pressing security issues. Though southeastern Arizona isn't a hawk migration corridor on par with Cape May, Hawk Mountain, or the Gulf Coast of Texas, every autumn brings a fair number and diversity of raptors passing through en route to milder climes. Grasshopper-eating Swainson's hawks are relatively harmless, but a southbound sharp-shinned or Cooper's with a grumbling gizzard might view our feeding station as a Stuckey's on the interstate and our granivorous clientele as feathered pecan logs. For the larger raptors, even the chickens are potential meals. That's why everyone was on guard that morning, from the tiniest goldfinch right up to me, the hens' devoted bodyguard.

As I watched Lucy luxuriating in a dust bath, a sudden chorus of alarm calls erupted and the feeder visitors dove for cover. Lucy froze, turned one eye to the sky, and let out a hoarse purr that means "raptor" in chicken lingo. I followed her gaze up and up to a distant but distinctive silhouette: a burly female peregrine falcon, scribing lazy circles against the cerulean sky. A conspicuous predator is seldom an immediate threat, but I kept an eye on both the chickens and the falcon until she soared off over the crest of a nearby hill. A quick check of eBird on my tablet confirmed that this was only the second peregrine for our yard list. (Cha-*ching!* Thanks, Lucy!)

Wherever you watch birds, and whatever birds you watch, it pays to study their calls and body language. Not only might they draw your attention to elusive species that you might otherwise miss, but you may find yourself in a front-row seat at one of nature's most compelling dramas. From a tiny hummingbird making threatening stabs toward the eyes of a roosting owl to a raucous flock of keel-billed toucans mobbing a black hawk-eagle as it rips shreds of meat from its prey, there's a lot to be gained from watching birds watch birds.

Even expert human hawk watchers can learn a thing or two from prey species. Picking out the field marks that distinguish a golden eagle from a dark-morph red-tailed hawk while it's still a half-mile away may earn you a new species for your yard, trip, year, or life list, but for sandhill cranes it may be a matter of life or death. When thousands of heads swivel in unison toward a speck on the horizon, that's your cue to take a closer look at the speck.

Watching southeastern Arizona's iconic vermilion flycatchers has taught us that males often perform their flamboyant "butterfly display" when they spot a raptor. It seems reckless for these already conspicuous birds to rise high over the trees, puff out their breasts, and flutter slowly through the air as if inviting attack, but maybe reckless is the whole point. Males that routinely challenge predators may appear as formidable territorial defenders to both potential mates and rivals.

One afternoon along the San Pedro River, a male vermilion flycatcher fluttered up against the blue sky, puffed out his brilliant red breast, and began his flight display. A quick

scan of the surroundings revealed only the silhouette of a turkey vulture approaching from the north. The vermilion continued his dance, bobbing and chirping like an animatronic Christmas ornament. As I smirked to myself at how this vigilant defender was wasting his time displaying over a harmless vulture, the silhouette continued its approach, closer and closer, until I finally noticed the feathered head and fearsomely taloned yellow feet of a zone-tailed hawk.

Raptors aren't always the villains in these scenarios. Generations of naturalists have reported small songbirds nesting close to large birds of prey, presumably gaining protection from their own predators at little risk to themselves. These relationships, called *protective associations*, are practical applications of the saying, "The enemy of my enemy is my friend."

A number of studies have uncovered distinct benefits for the less formidable members of these odd couples, including higher rates of nest success. A recent study found that for nesting female black-chinned hummingbirds, their worst enemies are egg-eating jays, and their best "frenemies" are jay-eating Cooper's hawks. Female hummingbirds that nested within a three-hundred-meter "no-fly zone" around hawks' nests had dramatically greater nesting success than those that nested farther away. The density of hummingbird nests also tended to be higher within this zone, which suggests that a good way to find hummingbird nests may be to look for hawk nests (or vice versa).

The protective association phenomenon may also explain why wind chimes and porch lights are such popular nest sites for some species of hummingbirds and why millions of blackbirds commute from communal roosts near urban centers to feeding areas in the countryside.

Birding is more than just identifying birds. It's finding them, watching them, and absorbing the lessons they can teach us about their species, their neighbors, and the world we share. Many of my most rewarding birding moments have come from flashes of insight into the minds of birds, gained by watching them interact with one another and their environment. Of the many mentors who have contributed to my growth as a birder, I owe the most to the ones on the other side of the binoculars.

TIPS
- For birds, spotting and identifying other birds can be a matter of life or death.
- Careful observation of even the most common birds can provide clues to the presence of both potential enemies and frenemies.
- Understanding the relationships between and among bird species and deciphering the messages in their calls and behaviors add depth and richness to the birding experience.

- When you're looking for mentors to help you improve your birding skills, remember that some of the best wear feathers.

S HERI L. WILLIAMSON, cofounder and director of the Southeastern Arizona Bird Observatory and author of the *Peterson Field Guide to Hummingbirds of North America,* has lived with and learned from birds for more than fifty years. She is fluent in several bird languages, including domestic chicken and eared quetzal.

YOUR AD HERE

Tech Birding

by Sharon Stiteler

WHEN I HEAR SOMEONE LAMENT THAT TECHNOLOGY IS ruining the outdoors, I roll my eyes. We live in an age of miracles, and technology makes it a fantastic time to be a birder and introduce people to the hobby.

As a kid growing up in Indiana, I did not have access to other birders. My mom tried her best to help me find birds, but there was no easy way to find out about a local bird club, what birds were being seen, or where bird walks happened. Even if we could find such things in the phone book or the newspaper, she was busy working full-time and taking care of her kids. Mom took me to parks when she could, but my birding consisted mostly of what was in our backyard and daydreaming over a National Geographic book called *The Wonder of Birds* that held tantalizing images. I wondered if I'd ever see things like trumpeter swans being reintroduced into Minnesota, sandhill cranes staging in Nebraska, or dozens of bald eagles roosting in trees next to a cold river.

I thought I was living the dream when, in my twenties, I worked full-time at a wild-bird-feed store. I had the *Sibley Guide to Birds* and both eastern and western CD sets of the *Stokes Field Guide to Bird Songs*. If I wanted to find out where birds were being seen and where bird clubs were meeting, I could use birding listservs. There were books written for most states with information on where to go birding. When I went out to the field, I would take a spotting scope, binoculars, digital camera, notebook, and a GPS unit to make sure I didn't get lost. I also kept a number of field guides and birding location guides in my car for reference.

The magic of today is filled with possibilities I wouldn't have understood as a kid. I have a camera that fits in my pocket, easily attaches to my spotting scope, and takes photos of birds that are print quality. The camera lets me store birding guides complete with songs, calls, and chip notes of most bird species found in North America. The camera also gives me driving directions and provides real-time weather and radar data in case a storm is coming. It lets me dictate notes, take a GPS point of where I saw a rare bird, and send messages to friends and groups about my sightings. I can enter checklists directly from the field, contributing to valuable citizen science data at the Cornell Lab of Ornithology. Oh yeah, and it takes phone calls, too. Thank you, iPhone.

The Internet and smartphones not only allow us to carry an unprecedented amount of information directly into the field, but they make birding more accessible. For years people thought birding was a not-very-exciting activity their grandmother did. Now, through the magic of social media on which people share their daily activities, an unprecedented number of nonbirders can be witness to people relaxing atop Canopy Tower in Panama, sipping gin and tonics while watching bat falcons fly overhead; or just-posted pictures of Finsch's wheatear outside a minefield in Israel; or birders celebrating with lifer pie, a fun tradition hatched at the Biggest Week in American Birding wherein birders celebrate seeing a new bird, such as a golden-winged warbler, with pie (or other tasty dessert of their choice).

Some of the most beloved field guides, such as the Sibley and National Geographic guides, have been converted into apps, reducing the amount of bulk people take out with them. There are apps just for specific groups, such as North American warblers or diurnal birds of prey, which can feature videos or 360-degree views of tricky species to help you learn how to tell them apart. If you are uncertain of a bird's identification, you can narrow your choices by setting the app for the location you are in, the habitat, and the time of year, and do smart searches using the bird's size, behavior, and noticeable field marks.

For the absolute beginning birder, there's the Merlin app, which asks a series of questions to help nonbirders—who may not be certain if something is a finch or a sparrow—identify new birds. The questions also help new birders figure out what to watch for when they see a new bird. There's even a website called BirdSnap that encourages people to submit photos of birds and the software will attempt to identify them. You can join groups on Facebook such as the American Birding Association's "What's this Bird?" Members and staff will help you identify your bird.

We have so many options to find birds now. The database eBird from the Cornell Lab of Ornithology is now global, and you can sign up for a free account to explore regions and hot spots on your computer; or you can get one of many apps such as BirdsEye, iBird, or the Audubon Bird Guide to see where birds are being reported near you. Some versions of the software will even use the navigation app that comes with your phone to give you driving directions to the spot.

If you are visiting another country, you can look for blogs and other social media accounts to see what people have found. A website called Birding Pal will hook you up with birders in your destination who can guide you and even let you crash at their home. There's also the option of all the different tour companies, who will tailor a trip to your brand of birding, such as hardcore listing in Ecuador, leisurely photography trips in Belize, or scotch distilleries and waterfowl in Scotland.

Documenting birds has never been easier. The eBird app will pinpoint your location and accept sightings of birds from the field. If you type in a rare bird, it will prompt you for notes to help confirm your observation. But reporting is not limited to birds. Project Noah and iNaturalist both take observations of all types of flora and fauna, and iNaturalist will even assign challenges, like having college students report dead birds on campus as a means of determining which buildings have the most lethal windows.

Technology is revolutionizing what we know about bird movement and how projects get funded. Project SnowStorm took advantage of an irruption of snowy owls in the winter of 2013–14. They used the GoFundMe platform to raise money from people interested in the project. The money was used to purchase satellite transmitters, which, attached to snowy owls, record real-time data of where the birds perch, fly, and breed.

Technology has been able to tell us where whimbrels migrate and how some will fly right into a hurricane and that they are susceptible to unregulated hunting in other countries. Radar can be used during migration to watch for night migrants and, as in Israel, to identify large flocks of cranes, storks, and pelicans to help pilots avoid collisions.

This is not to say that technology is turning everyone into perfect birders and solving all of our conservation problems. But if technology is getting anyone of any age interested in the birds around them and helping them, then I'm all for it. Where will we go from here? I'm excited to find out.

TIPS

- Don't assume technology is ruining the outdoors. It's a great way to bridge the gap with young people and get them interested.
- If you have a question, try typing it into a search engine like Google before you ask a birding group.
- If you need to know the identification of something, try posting it to an online group with a guess. People are far more likely to correct a misidentification than to answer the question, "What is this?"

SHARON STITELER saw a Peterson Field Guide when she was seven, and she snapped. Since 1997 she's made her goal to get paid to go birding, which has led to an eclectic career of writing, speaking at bird festivals, doing radio and television segments, conducting bird surveys, and leading bird tours. Her books include *Disapproving Rabbits* and *1001 Secrets Every Birder Should Know.* You can find her on most social media as Birdchick.

Birding Champagne

by Rick Wright

I DON'T KNOW ANYONE WHO EVER HAS ENOUGH TIME. OUR days are filled and overfilled with jobs, families, pets, and property, and no matter how happily we attend to them, those duties and the hustle-bustle of the rest of our daily obligations leave us precious few moments to indulge in other, less urgent pursuits.

When we finally do manage to cobble together the time—a day, a week—to devote to leisure, we birders are faced with another dilemma: we are, on the whole, interesting people and interested, with a vast range of backgrounds and passions. Birders may be famously obsessive, but our urgent dedication to things feathered is not, for most of us, the same as single-mindedness. We in the binoculared crowd throw ourselves with the same overwhelming gusto into everything that fascinates us, whether it's beer or botany, baking or Brahms.

So how do we make the hard choice between one hobby and another?

The secret: we birders don't have to.

I like to think of birding as the champagne of hobbies. That claim may sound snooty; it may raise some eyebrows. But like the bubbly white wine of northeastern France, birding can be costly or not. It can be a casual bit of fun or a demanding exercise in connoisseurship, and it can most certainly be intoxicating. It is often enjoyed with the assistance of unnecessarily expensive glass. Most of all, though, birding, just like champagne, goes with absolutely any other activity. As a famous old optics ad would have it, most of us are never *not* birding.

For example, anyone with the slightest, most dimly remembered knowledge of art will jump at the chance to visit Florence, Venice, or Paris. Birders, too; but our experience is twice as rich when we find black redstarts singing their gritty grumbles from the façade of the Louvre, great cormorants splashing and diving ahead of the water taxis on the Venetian Lagoon, and peregrine falcons soaring and squawking over Giotto's perfect bell tower. If the galleries of the Uffizi overwhelm, as they invariably do, we simply turn from the Leonardos and the Titians to gaze out the window at the egrets, wagtails, and sandpipers haunting the banks of the Arno below. In the Provençal asylum of Saint-Paul de Mausole, where Vincent van Gogh lived and painted for most of the last year of his short life, the windows have bars—but beneath them the irises still bloom, and buntings, titmice, and warblers fill

the lavender-scented air with their incongruously lively trills and whistles.

More ancient ruins, too, from the Greek outposts of Catalonia and Provence to Jordan's glorious Petra, are all the more evocative for those of us who know that the thrushes and finches are the descendants of birds that haunted those timeless stones centuries before us. As the same yellow-legged gulls and common terns circle and fish in the wine-red sea, we can almost hear the slapping of oars and the shouts from the galleys approaching cities that declined and vanished in a millennium not our own. To walk through a Roman triumphal arch while hoopoes hoot and rollers flash past to out-blue the blue sky is to experience antiquity in a way no nonbirder ever could, and the Etruscan tombs of Vulci are made even more poignant by the bee-eaters that have dug their nest holes into the tufa walls, bringing forth new life every year in a place meant only for the dead.

More recent landscapes have their ornithological charms, too. In easternmost Austria, great bitterns and European spoonbills lurk in the reeds not far from the country houses and palaces where Haydn performed for galant audiences. Wallcreepers winter on the stern walls of the fortress above the Salzburg block where Mozart was born, and nightingales and cuckoos still sing from the Vienna Woods, just as they did two centuries ago when Beethoven was composing his sixth symphony during long walks along the quiet paths.

Less cerebral pursuits also benefit from their combination with birding. From Szechuan to Santiago, the pilgrimage routes trod by the "foodies" are lined with birds. There is no more perfect day in France than one that begins with the herons and flamingos of the Camargue marshes, followed by a pensive afternoon's stroll through the two-thousand-year-old necropolis of the Arlesian Alyscamps—and ending with a fine but simple Provençal meal on a summer-warmed terrace, where the air is filled with the scent of lavender and jasmine and the ear with the wild keening of the blackbirds.

Landscapes known for their food are often equally famous for their wine. The vineyards of British Columbia's Okanagan Valley not only produce some of the best grapes in the world, but also serve as home to mountain bluebirds, western kingbirds, and western meadowlarks; birders enjoy their well-earned glass even more when the label on the bottle is adorned by the same burrowing owls they watched that morning. In Burgundy, cirl buntings and bee-eaters perch and hunt from the stakes supporting the vines on the flinty slopes, and the sunny side of the valley of the Mosel draws clownish hoopoes and glistening kingfishers as surely as it does human oenophiles of taste and discernment. In Chile, Argentina, Italy, Hungary, and dozens of other destinations, the wine and the birds compete at first for our attention—until we relent and enjoy both equally.

To the outsider, birding tourism can sometimes seem

drearily single-minded, the twitching and ticking of birds that are ultimately little more than names on a field guide page. But birding travelers who approach each new landscape as a fine-woven tissue of human tradition and natural abundance, a seamless blend of culture, history, and the living environment, find a new depth to each destination; they discover satisfying connections and puzzling conjunctions, and return from the field each evening with a more profound sense of how they and their fellows might fit into the created and cultural world around them.

TOP PICKS

- The warm, dry climate of British Columbia's Okanagan Valley is just right for white-throated swifts, canyon wrens, and the grapes that go into some of the best wines in the Americas.
- In Cambridge, Massachusetts, historic Mount Auburn Cemetery is the resting place of famous artists, philosophers, and ornithologists—and of tired northbound warblers every spring.
- The Classical Mayan city of Tikal is the best place in the world to see the rare orange-breasted falcon and many other colorful tropical birds.
- Alaska's Aleutian Islands, site of some of the bloodiest battles of World War II, are now "invaded" every year by birders in search of rare Asian strays.

- The Romanesque monasteries of Burgundy are a peaceful refuge for the descendants of birds that watched their construction nearly a millennium ago.

A native of southeast Nebraska, RICK WRIGHT holds the M.A. and Ph.D. in German from Princeton University. His years as an academic included appointments as assistant professor of German at the University of Illinois, reader/scholar at Princeton University's Index of Christian Art, and associate professor of medieval studies at Fordham University. He leads Birds and Art tours for Victor Emanuel Nature Tours, and writes obsessively about the history and culture of birders and birding.

Why I'm a Patch Birder

by Charles Hagner

I AM A LUCKY GUY. MY FAVORITE BIRDING HOT SPOT, Estabrook Park, is just a five-minute walk from my back door.

It's a county park, situated along the east bank of the Milwaukee River in Milwaukee County, Wisconsin, one of a dozen or so green spaces that Charles B. Whitnall and other far-sighted city planners plotted out in the early 1920s to serve as the lungs of a fast-growing metropolis, breathing spots open to every citizen. Parks would aid the cause of civilization, Whitnall believed, by "conserving those environmental influences which park experts recognize as essential to wholesome living conditions."*

He drafted his master plan at a time when it was still possible to chat with Milwaukeeans who remembered the abundance of environmental influences bestowed by the county in the mid-1800s, before settlement and rapid urbanization.

---

* As quoted in *The Making of Milwaukee*, by John Gurda (Milwaukee County Historical Society, 1999 and 2006), p. 270.

Then, upland woods (oaks, sugar maples, beech, basswood, hickories) covered no less than 84 percent of the land. Canada and black-throated green warblers nested in ravines in the bluffs overlooking the Lake Michigan shoreline. Flocks of "prairie hen" (greater prairie-chicken and sharp-tailed grouse) were spotted from coaches and trains. And each winter, migratory wildfowl gathered by the thousands in wetlands at the confluence of the Menomonee, Kinnickinnic, and Milwaukee Rivers, at what would become the heart of the city. Even more astonishing, Carolina parakeet was an occasional summer wanderer, and passenger pigeon, another soon-to-be-extinct species, migrated along the lakeshore.

By 2001, when I moved to the area to become the editor of *BirdWatching* magazine, almost all of the native plant habitats in the county were long gone. Where upland woods had once stood, there were roads, buildings, and more buildings. According to the Southeastern Wisconsin Regional Planning Commission, no less than 89.6 percent of the county was classified as residential, commercial, industrial, or institutional, and ecologists said less than 2 percent of the remaining habitat, almost all of it in parks, was of any quality. The lungs of the city were needed more than ever.

Less than half a mile wide and a mile and a half long, Estabrook is a narrow park, bounded on its long sides by the Milwaukee River and residential areas and on the north and south by multilane thoroughfares. Two-lane Estabrook Drive splits it lengthwise into even narrower sections, and a popular bike path, paved walkways, and mountain-bike trails subdivide it further. Consequently, it lacks vegetated areas large enough to attract and sustain wood thrush, scarlet tanager, and other species that nest in forest interiors, but Baltimore orioles weave dangling nests in its trees each summer and common goldeneyes display on the river every winter.

In 2000, the Wisconsin Society for Ornithology, in the fourth edition of its essential bird-finding guide, *Wisconsin's Favorite Bird Haunts,* described the park as "great for birding." The designation was thanks largely to the river, which serves as a guiding line for northward-migrating Nearctic/Neotropical species. They fly at night, often great distances, and most individuals stop frequently during the day to rest and refuel, putting down in almost any conceivable shelter. Scientists say urban swatches containing even small amounts of low-quality vegetation are valuable, since they enable birds simply to survive, so they can continue migrating another day.

Yet when the fifth edition of *Bird Haunts* appeared in 2009, Estabrook was left out, as were two other county parks that had been featured in the previous edition. Looking back, I realize I should have seen the omission coming: as budgets tightened, the county had put off maintenance. Graffiti hadn't been removed, and garlic mustard had spread. "Unsavory characters" were rumored to frequent the park. What's more, new birding haunts had been discovered elsewhere in the state. They deserved write-ups, too, the book's editor told me; there wasn't room for everything.

Still, the thought that neighbors of mine might be staying away from my park bothered me. I had walked its paths safely for years, filling notebooks with the arrival and departure dates of warblers and other birds that build their nests far to my north and spend the winter far to my south. Witnessing their annual movements had been a mostly solitary pursuit, a personal pleasure, an opportunity to concentrate on the planet's grand natural calendar rather than the magazine's bimonthly production schedule, but now it dawned on me that my bird watching could serve a practical purpose, perhaps even inject a bit of fresh air into century-old lungs.

I became a patch birder. I started bird watching in Estabrook Park every weekend, all year round, and reporting my sightings to eBird, the real-time online checklist operated by the Cornell Lab of Ornithology and Audubon. More important, playing a hunch that the presence of birds might make a community think again about a park that had fallen out of mind, I made it a point to share what I had seen—via an email listserv, on Facebook, and at meetings of a park friends group that I helped found.

When I started, few administrators of the village I live in had any idea that so many different birds relied on the park. I've since recorded over 160 bird species, most of them during spring and fall, or in winter, when small numbers of ducks, including the goldeneyes, make do on unfrozen sections of the river. My regular monitoring helped the village satisfy requirements for certification as a bird-friendly community via the innovative Bird City Wisconsin program, and I'm no longer the only birder reporting sightings in Estabrook, a result that has me musing about the sixth edition of *Wisconsin's Favorite Bird Haunts.* But it's the indirect results of my patch birding that are most satisfying.

The park is once again functioning as the city planners intended it, as a breathing spot open to every citizen. Thanks to the creativity of volunteer groups and the cooperation of the county, it recently gained a dog-exercise area and then a disc golf course. Thanks to the hard work of the friends group—we've been planting trees, organizing cleanups, and removing buckthorn and garlic mustard—the park is looking better. And in 2012, an outdoor beer garden opened, the first in Milwaukee since Prohibition, Whitnall's era. I'm sure its proprietors had their choice of locations to offer their giant pretzels and infectious oom-pah-pah music, but they went where there were birds. Prost!

TIPS

- Find a local patch near you and bird it regularly throughout the year. Your sightings will heighten your enjoyment of the changing seasons and make it easier to recognize rarities.

- Keep track of what you see, and report your sightings on eBird. Your records will help scientists monitor the distribution and abundance of birds continent-wide, and the data will serve as a yardstick you can use to assess the effects, positive and negative, of future changes made to your patch.

- Share your sightings. Don't assume your neighbors already know how important your local patch is to resident and migratory birds. They may have no idea.

CHARLES HAGNER is the editor in chief of bimonthly *BirdWatching* magazine, the author of two books about birds and birding, and a director of the Western Great Lakes Bird and Bat Observatory in southeastern Wisconsin. He has birded Estabrook Park regularly for over eight years.

I Love Birding Because
It Gets Me Closer to Tacos

by Nick Lund

A S AN OYSTERCATCHER NEEDS OYSTERS, AS A SAPSUCKER needs sap, as a flycatcher needs flies, I need burritos. To say that I like Mexican cuisine is an understatement. I *need* it. An ornithologist would call me a "specialist," with a diet confined to a narrow set of ingredients: tortillas, ground meat, cheese, tomatoes, onions, avocados, beans, hot sauce, salsa, spices.

I'm not entirely sure how it got like this. Growing up in Maine, before I was a birder, I certainly wasn't exposed to great Mexican cuisine. Like a hummingbird drinking artificial red syrup out of a hanging feeder, I made do with what I could find. Sometimes it was a trip to Margaritas in downtown Portland to eat beans smothered in Jack cheese and drink virgin cocktails out of a cactus-shaped glass. More often it was a pilgrimage to the Maine Mall to stop at Taco Bell—the only one in the state at the time—to load up on whatever godforsaken

creation they were slopping together that month. Still, without ever having anything better, I savored every bite.

My current home of Washington, D.C., though light-years ahead of what I grew up with in Maine, is still no mecca for quality Mexican food. For the good stuff I need to head south.

Thankfully, annual birding trips within the ABA area regularly take me to where Mexican food is cooked with a level of care and craftsmanship impossible to find in the Northeast. On those trips, in the midst of my temporary southbound migration, the discovery of a good burrito is as memorable as the life birds I've ostensibly come to find. In fact, just hearing the name of certain species evokes sense-memories that include the taste of refried beans and the floury touch of a fresh tortilla

Let me share some of those delicious memories with you.

We found just about all of our target birds on my first trip to southeastern Arizona. My friend Jake and I would leave early each morning from our home base in Tucson, find all the birds we could, then return at the end of the day, exhausted, to the first Mexican restaurant we could find. After a day scouring Mount Lemmon, finding greater pewees, buff-bellied flycatchers, and red-faced warblers, we celebrated with carne seca, a local specialty, in a tiny place downtown with a name I can't remember, if I ever knew it to begin with. Two other nights we returned to the city and ate Sonoran hot dogs at El Güero Canelo, and dared each other to eat hotter and hotter peppers.

California has more variety. I ate fish tacos at Point Loma Seafoods in San Diego after seeing my first albatross offshore. My six-hundredth ABA bird was a gray vireo up Kitchen Creek Road; our group celebrated by passing around a bottle of tequila (not Mexican food per se, but in the same spirit) and watching the sunset over the Pacific. Best of all was another no-name joint, somewhere just south of the Salton Sea (Calipatria? Niland?) where the chorizo-and-egg tacos were cheap and we plowed across the language barrier to talk with the owner about eagles (all nonbirders like to talk with birders about eagles).

Even Alaska has good Mexican food. Alaska! One of my favorite small chains in the country is the Taco Kings in Anchorage. I ate there several times on my last trip north, rapidly replenishing calories burned chasing ptarmigan and northern wheatear up the Arctic Valley Ski Area.

And then there's Texas. Big, beautiful Texas. Birds have brought me to points all along the Texas–Mexico border, and I've celebrated each one with memorable food. I spent my first day in El Paso at the L&J Cafe, and celebrated my lifer Colima warbler with prickly pear margaritas at the Starlight Theatre in Terlingua. Where I'm from, the only food you can get at gas stations are red hot dogs fished out of a steamer tank, but in Texas I ate three meals a day—with freshly made tortillas!—at the Laredo Taco Company outposts that are found in every Stripes station.

The most memorable meals are the unexpected ones. Our party was desperate for a meal after a hot afternoon spent looking unsuccessfully for ringed kingfisher along a dusty canal outside the town of Santa Maria. We pulled into the first place we saw with a "tacos" sign out front. It was a place called the Road Side Inn, in the town of Hidalgo, and we walked in just as the kitchen was closing. A guy came out from the back, apologizing for things shutting down, and offered us the last of whatever they had: some fresh corn tortillas, a spicy red sauce, and a big chunk of the most delicious mystery meat any of us had ever eaten. We set up shop on a bench out front, drinking ice-cold Lone Stars, and couldn't believe our luck as we giddily filled tortilla after tortilla.

One of the many reasons I love birding is because it's brought me closer to delicious Mexican food. Another reason I love birding is that there's no rush. I'm still considered a young birder, and because birding is probably the lowest-impact outdoor hobby, I've got plenty of years left for birding to bring me to new cuisines. I'm looking forward to one place in particular, a place with a ton of great birds and a lot of great Mexican food: Mexico. Everything I've eaten so far could probably be more accurately described as "Tex-Mex," and I'm no stickler for whatever "authenticity" purports to be anyway, but my mouth waters just thinking about what will be on my plate after a long day chasing trogons and toucans and everything else down there. I'll get there someday. Until then, *mas tequila!*

TIPS for Finding Good Mexican Food While Birding

- Leave the white linen napkins at home. Most of the best food I've had has been from places that weren't exactly the Ritz; some of them barely even advertised that they sold food. It doesn't matter. If it looks good and smells good, it'll be good.
- If you don't know Spanish, just point and nod. I am dumb and don't know how to speak anything but English, and in many cases the folks I was ordering from spoke only Spanish. It doesn't matter. Just do the best you can with pronunciation, and don't worry too much if you don't end up with exactly what you thought you were getting.
- Don't forget about breakfast! I grew up thinking that Mexican food was just an evening thing, but starting off your day with *huevos* and beans is as good as it gets.

▷▷●◁◁

NICK LUND lives in Washington, D.C., and is the author of the website The Birdist. He writes a weekly column for the National Audubon Society called "The Birdist's Rules of Birding" and also regularly contributes to Slate.com, *National Parks* magazine, and other outlets.

Driving Miss Phoebe
(OR, IN THE COMPANY OF RED-TAILS)

by Julie Zickefoose

NORMALLY, IT'S ONEROUS TO LIVE TWO HOURS FROM THE nearest airport, especially for frequent travelers like us. But when your daughter has been home for a blinding-fast month from college on winter break, and you dread sending her back to Maine, so very far away from Ohio, that two-hour drive is a beautiful thing.

As the time for her departure grew near, I'd see the thought of leaving cross her mind. It was as if a cloud had sailed across the sun, darkening her clear blue eyes. I was busy the last evening she was home, and didn't have time to fix one of her favorite meals, defaulting to a quasi-Indian stir-fry. As she was poking her fork into it, a tear slid down her nose. "I'm sorry this isn't your favorite, honey. Plus, it has rice, and I know you don't like rice." Phoebe burst out laughing and weeping at the same time. "It's fine! It just occurred to me that this is my last dinner at home."

"I know."

"It's good. It really is. It's not about the rice." We wiped tears and laughed as we finished an anticlimactic stir-fry.

So I was dreading the parting, but looking forward to those last two hours together, after she'd said goodbye to the dog, kissing his graying muzzle and frosty eyebrows again and again; after she'd wheeled her suitcases down the sidewalk. We wound along the ridgetop toward the highway, looking at the rare winter sun stroking the Appalachian foothills. It felt like an auspicious day, a day of new horizons. That morning, Phoebe had spotted an adult red-shouldered hawk sitting in a wild pear just outside the studio where she and I were discussing what she might do in the coming summer. The hawk was so big, so close and so beautiful, its breast mottled in burnt orange and white. It took off for the orchard as soon as I got binoculars on it, its work done. I hadn't seen that bird in the yard at all this winter, and I marveled that it chose this day to appear. The red-shoulder is my late father's hawk of choice, the one he sends when he wants us to know he's near and keeping watch over us. But he's liable to steer other species our way as well; just the day before, an out-of-habitat northern harrier had tip-tilted over our car, bringing squeals of joy and surprise from Phoebe and me at seeing this open-country bird in a narrow bottomland hayfield close to home.

We rolled along the ridge, scanning the land one last time. A kestrel teetered on a phone wire, and then we spotted another, and in a moment of inspiration, I suggested to Phoebe that we keep count of all the raptors we would see on the two-hour, 135-mile drive to the airport. She grabbed a pen and a tissue box to write on and resumed combing the landscape with sharp young eyes while I drove. Because I-77 runs through largely agricultural land, with pasture and hayfield opening up the rolling oak-hickory woodlands, the red-tailed hawk is king. Better yet, it was a cold but sunny day, the first decent soaring day in an otherwise sodden week. Red-tails dotted the waysides, their cream-white bellies turned toward the sun. January 20, and they were almost all paired up already! Many times, I'd spot one, and at the same instant Phoebe would find its mate. We'd exchange hurried descriptions to make sure we were looking at different birds, and in this way we swiftly doubled our numbers: eight, ten, twelve, counting by twos.

As we rolled along, we talked and laughed, occasionally reaching out to squeeze each other's hands. As much as I loved that round and baldish baby, her red hair in a Kewpie twist, her blue eyes wise beyond their months; as much as I loved that toddler in the shopping cart, smiling up at me through a mouth full of crackers; there's nothing quite like the companionship of a daughter who's grown up fair and

wise and funny, too. She's suddenly an adult, riding shotgun; finishing my wandering sentences, completing my thoughts, firing bright flashes of wisdom and insight.

And the hawks kept coming, perched in oaks and topping telephone poles, skirts of feathers spreading out like fluffy pantaloons on either side of craggy yellow feet. A yearling red-tail straddled prey in the median strip, crown feathers lifted like an angry god, yellow eyes blazing as it squeezed some small life into oblivion. "These hawks have highway living figured out. You don't see near as many of them hit as you should, given their numbers," I commented. These visions swept into our minds and just as quickly blew out as the cruise control held a steady seventy. We were watching a bird filmstrip, catching eyefuls as we rolled.

We approached Caldwell, Ohio, where for the past four years we have occasionally seen a pure white red-tail, a female, we guess, by the looks of her smaller, normally pigmented mate. Phoebe always remembers to watch for her, remembers the exact tree where we saw her last. "We have to watch for the white red-tail!" she said, and against all odds and right on cue I picked up a distant white blotch that looked like a bit of snow caught in a forked branch. The rumble strip sang as I pulled over and dug out my car binoculars. Dense and heavy as a small brick, the Zeiss 8 power compact is thirty-three years old, with the indestructibility required of an instrument consigned to a car. Phoebe and I shared slightly schmutzy binocular views of this apparition, this spirit hawk who appears or (mostly) doesn't. Her dark eyes glowed like coals against her spotless plumage as she relaxed high in a tree. Her much smaller mate beat his way across the four-lane in a direct line to her as we pulled back onto the highway. Wahoo! Double hawk-score!

By the time we neared I-270, the madly rushing beltway around Columbus, our numbers were in the forties. Red-shoulders, two; kestrels, five; one hard-flapping Cooper's hawk; and thirty-six red-tails, a staggering count for a two-hour drive. Housing developments and shopping centers took over in beltway sprawl, and Phoebe remarked that we may have found all the red-tails we were going to find. "Well, red-tails love airports, so don't give up hope," I replied, taking the back approach for its wide grassland habitat. Phoebe narrowed her pale blue eyes—my father's eyes—her head turning ceaselessly. *Like a Cooper's hawk,* I thought, sneaking a glance at her, *sharp as a blade,* as I rounded a curve. And perched on a chainlink fence just a few feet off Phoebe's window was an enormous female red-tail, every detail of her streaked front, yellow feet, and shining bill roaring into naked-eye focus. We broke into a whoop of victory and a spontaneous high-five as our raptor count hit forty-five.

The inevitable airport curbside good-bye; the air, as always, tinged with the smoke of passengers' last discarded cigarettes, left rolling and smoking on the sidewalk as people enter the terminal. It's never my favorite part of the trip. But nothing could dim the glow of those two hawk-sweetened hours, driving Miss Phoebe to her next semester and thence to her wonderful life. The watching red-shoulder; the fierce god in the median; the big white spirit hawk; the lady bruiser on the chainlink as a grand finale: riches and miracles, each one. We'd made the trip with love and style, birding all the way. And I know as Phoebe moves forward into her new life, she'll be ever watchful and appreciative, and always in the company of red-tails.

TIPS for Birding with Your Kids

- Take them along from an early age, bringing awesome snacks they get only while birding.
- Give them decent optics from the start. Would *you* want to bird through toy binoculars?
- Dedicate a field guide just to your child. Seeing it get dog-eared is the whole point.
- Always honor a child's plea to come see something she's found outdoors. This will tell her that noticing nature is worth jumping up for.
- Hope the love for birding rubs off on them, but don't push if it doesn't.

>>•<<

JULIE ZICKEFOOSE'S most recent book, from Houghton Mifflin Harcourt, is *Baby Birds: An Artist Looks into the Nest*. Painting nestlings from hatching through fledging has proven addictive, and the perfect dovetail with her continuing avian rehabilitation work. She has found other callings in leading birding trips abroad, and loping along dirt roads in her beloved Appalachian Ohio foothills, taking photos and sharing them on her blog since 2009.

INDEX